The California Gold Rush

A Brief History with Documents

D0218185

THE BEDFORD SERIES IN HISTORY AND CULTURE

The California Gold Rush
A Brief History with Documents

Andrew C. Isenberg

Temple University

bedford/st.martin's
Macmillan Learning

Boston | New York

For Bedford/St. Martin's

Vice President, Editorial, Macmillan Learning Humanities: Edwin Hill
Program Director for History: Michael Rosenberg
Senior Program Manager for History: William J. Lombardo
History Marketing Manager: Melissa Rodriguez
Director of Content Development: Jane Knetzger
Assistant Editor: Melanie McFadyen
Associate Editor: Mary Posman Starowicz
Content Project Manager: Lidia MacDonald-Carr
Senior Workflow Project Manager: Lisa McDowell
Production Supervisor: Robert Cherry
Media Project Manager: Michelle Camisa
Manager of Publishing Services: Andrea Cava
Project Management: Lumina Datamatics, Inc.
Composition: Lumina Datamatics, Inc.
Cartographer: Mapping Specialists, Ltd.
Director of Rights and Permissions: Hilary Newman
Permissions Manager: Kalina Ingham
Senior Art Director: Anna Palchik
Cover Design: William Boardman
Cover Photo: (front cover) Spencer Weiner/Getty Images; (back cover) Elena Isenberg
Printing and Binding: LSC Communications

Manufactured in the United States of America.

2 1 0 9 8 7
f e d c b a

For information, write: Bedford/St. Martin's, 75 Arlington Street, Boston, MA 02116

ISBN 978-1-4576-7164-7

Acknowledgments
Acknowledgments and copyrights appear on the same page as the text and art selections they cover; these acknowledgments and copyrights constitute an extension of the copyright page.

At the time of publication all Internet URLs published in this text were found to accurately link to their intended website. If you do find a broken link, please forward the information to history@macmillan.com so that it can be corrected for the next printing.

Foreword

The Bedford Series in History and Culture is designed so that readers can study the past as historians do.

The historian's first task is finding the evidence. Documents, letters, memoirs, interviews, pictures, movies, novels, or poems can provide facts and clues. Then the historian questions and compares the sources. There is more to do than in a courtroom, for hearsay evidence is welcome, and the historian is usually looking for answers beyond act and motive. Different views of an event may be as important as a single verdict. How a story is told may yield as much information as what it says.

Along the way the historian seeks help from other historians and perhaps from specialists in other disciplines. Finally, it is time to write, to decide on an interpretation and how to arrange the evidence for readers.

Each book in this series contains an important historical document or group of documents, each document a witness from the past and open to interpretation in different ways. The documents are combined with some element of historical narrative — an introduction or a biographical essay, for example — that provides students with an analysis of the primary source material and important background information about the world in which it was produced.

Each book in the series focuses on a specific topic within a specific historical period. Each provides a basis for lively thought and discussion about several aspects of the topic and the historian's role. Each is short enough (and inexpensive enough) to be a reasonable one-week assignment in a college course. Whether as classroom or personal reading, each book in the series provides firsthand experience of the challenge — and fun — of discovering, re-creating, and interpreting the past.

Lynn Hunt
David W. Blight
Bonnie G. Smith

Preface

In 1848, few Americans—few people *anywhere*—knew much about California. It was a remote, underpopulated, largely agrarian province that Mexico had recently ceded to the United States at the end of a brief war. The discovery of gold in early 1848 on the American River, roughly midway between San Francisco Bay and the Sierra Nevada, changed California's fate. Suddenly, this previously unremarkable place mattered. By the end of 1849, 100,000 people had flooded into California, almost all of them in search of a fortune; by the end of 1850, California had joined the Union. Most of the migrants to California failed to become wealthy, but as a whole in the early 1850s, California produced one-third of the gold in the world.

We tend to remember the California Gold Rush as a pleasant adventure. Both the aggregate wealth that the Gold Rush produced and the rapid incorporation of a former Mexican province into the United States have fueled the sense that the California Gold Rush was a story of ready wealth and the facile realization of national ambitions. The search for gold itself is often told as a happy, almost comic story: Some prospectors struck it rich, while others failed with good humor. We rehearse that narrative at nostalgia sites like amusement parks that invite visitors to pan for gold in a trough filled with sand and water.

Yet, as the Introduction in Part One of this volume clarifies, the Gold Rush was as chaotic as it was sudden. It was, first of all, characterized by appalling violence. White prospectors sought to drive Chinese, African American, and Latin American competitors from the gold fields. The worst violence was perpetrated against Native Americans, whose population in California fell from roughly 150,000 in 1848 to about 30,000 in 1870. The environmental effects of gold mining were devastating. Although the Gold Rush is memorialized with the simple technique of panning, by the mid-1850s industrial techniques such as hydraulic mining were in ascendancy. Hydraulic hoses carved enormous craters in the gold country and fouled and clogged streams with debris.

The documents in Part Two of this collection confront these controversies and paradoxes of the Gold Rush directly. The collection focuses on the social and environmental context and consequences of the Gold Rush, and considers whether the popular memory and scholarly understanding of the Gold Rush reflects that context and those consequences.

The first section of Part Two considers some of the early reactions to the discovery of gold, and, within a few years, the observations of several new Californians that finding wealth in the gold fields was not as simple as they had been led to believe. Many moved on to other endeavors, collecting in burgeoning cities, which is the subject of the second section. Those cities were, like prospecting for gold, speculative enterprises. They were founded by merchants who hoped to make their fortunes in real estate rather than in mining. Some cities failed. The largest—San Francisco and Sacramento—experienced explosive violence between factions that battled for control of the cities.

The third section places California both in national and transnational context. When California sought admission to the Union in 1849, it thrust itself into national political disputes over slavery. It was eventually admitted, as part of the Compromise of 1850, as a large free state in the West to balance the 1845 admission of Texas, a large slave state in the West. Yet slavery persisted in California throughout the 1850s. The Gold Rush was also a transnational event. Tens of thousands of gold-seekers came to California from outside the United States. Before the 1850s were over, tens of thousands of Americans would leave California to join gold rushes in Australia and British Columbia.

The fourth, fifth, and sixth sections consider the impact of the Gold Rush on non-whites in California: the Californios who had dominated Mexican California before the discovery of gold; the Native Americans who were displaced and murdered; and the Chinese who were relegated to subordinate status in a state in which the privileges of white laborers were considered paramount. The seventh section considers the effects of industrial techniques of gold mining on the environment.

Finally, the last section briefly surveys the work of three historians of the 1880s and 1890s who painted the Gold Rush in largely positive terms, erasing ethnic violence and environmental costs.

ACKNOWLEDGMENTS

I am grateful to Senior Program Manager for History William Lombardo, who first suggested to me that I might put together a collection of documents on the California Gold Rush, and to Melanie McFadyen and Mary Posman Starowicz for their help in honing the collection. I would also like to thank the following from Bedford/St. Martin's: Program Director for History Michael Rosenberg, History Marketing Manager Melissa Rodriguez, Cover Designer William Boardman, and Content Project Manager Lidia MacDonald-Carr. Carrie Alexander and Jordan Keagle tracked down documents for me at the California State Library, the Bancroft Library, and the Huntington Library; I am deeply grateful to them for their help. I received detailed and helpful critiques from a number of scholars, including Kevin Adams, Kent State University; Douglas Dodd, California State University Bakersfield; Philip Garone, California State University Stanislaus; Lee Simpson, California State University Sacramento; and Ashley Riley Sousa, Middle Tennessee State University. Together, they spared me from several mistakes and nudged the collection in fruitful directions. Any factual or interpretive errors that remain are entirely my responsibility.

Andrew C. Isenberg

Contents

Map

PART ONE

Introduction:
Race, Property, and the
California Gold Rush

The story of the California Gold Rush is one of unanticipated, rapid, and momentous change. James Marshall's discovery of gold on the South Fork of the American River (Map 1) in January 1848 set in motion a transformative series of events that brought 100,000 argonauts to California by the end of 1849. California became the thirty-first state just a year later. Because the discovery of gold occurred just as Mexico ceded California to the United States after the conclusion of a two-year-long war, many interpreters have integrated the California Gold Rush into a story of American national expansion. Yet that outcome was not foreordained. Throughout the 1840s, American immigrants in California seriously envisioned the possibility of an independent state modeled on the Republic of Texas.[1] Many of the first American emigrants to California were Mormons who imagined that California might be an outpost of a larger Mormon polity centered in the Great Basin.[2] After 1861, a number of prominent Californians hoped to make California part of the Confederacy.[3] Moreover, the Gold Rush was in many respects a transnational phenomenon: the gold country drew prospectors from Latin America, Europe, and Asia as well as from the eastern United States. Many American gold-seekers in the 1850s quickly left California for newly-discovered gold fields in Australia, British Columbia, and elsewhere.

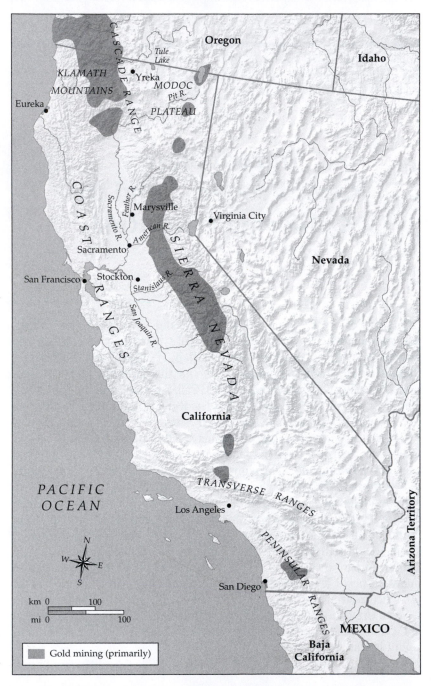

Map 1. *The California Gold Country, 1848–1884*

While the rapid admission of California to the United States makes its integration into the American political system seem smooth, statehood merely imposed a thin veneer of stability. Beneath the surface, turmoil reigned. Prospectors in California improvised mining regulations and readily formed themselves into mining companies.[4] Yet in other ways social stability, self-governance, and the rule of law were elusive: conflict and violence between squatters and landholders, native-born whites and Asian or Latin American immigrants, vigilantes and their victims, and not least of all between prospectors and Indians, punctuated the period following the discovery of gold. Non white immigrants, squatters, and Indians received the worst in these conflicts. Indeed, a number of scholars have aptly described the destruction of California Indians as genocide.[5] California produced enormous wealth in the two decades following the initial discovery of gold. That bullion helped to finance the Union cause in the American Civil War and the American industrial takeoff in the second half of the nineteenth century. Yet gold mining exacted steep environmental costs. Altogether, the California Gold Rush is one of the most memorialized events in American history. Yet its larger meaning remains unresolved and controversial.

BEFORE THE GOLD RUSH

Prior to the arrival of Europeans in the Americas, California was one of the most densely-populated areas north of Mexico. At least 300,000 natives inhabited California prior to Spanish colonization. The population of pre contact California was not only dense but diverse: over one hundred separate ethnicities, speaking no fewer than sixty different languages belonging to five major Native American language groups. One might expect such a dense and diverse population to rely primarily on agriculture, like the Algonquian, Iroquoian, and Muskogean groups of eastern North America. Yet in California, natives took advantage of the density and diversity of resources to rely on a combination of fishing, hunting, and gathering. Such a resource strategy required careful management; the combination of fishing, hunting, and gathering usually provides a stable source of subsistence only for dispersed populations that can draw on resources over a broad area. Indians of California set low-intensity forest fires in the fall and spring to clear underbrush and to promote the growth of new shoots that attracted browsing animals such as deer. On the coast, in the valleys, and in the foothills of the Sierra Nevada, Indians harvested acorns every autumn in order to process them into flour. For natives living along the Klamath-Trinity and

Sacramento-San Joaquin river systems (the second- and third-largest
river systems on the Pacific coast of North America south of Puget
Sound), the seasonal harvest of salmon as the fish made their way
upstream to spawn was the primary source of subsistence.[6]

Yet fires sometimes escaped the Indians' superintendence, destroying
large swaths of forest. Archeological evidence suggests that some coastal
communities overharvested shellfish and subsequently had to abandon
their coastal settlements. Roughly 800 years before the discovery of gold,
overhunting may have depressed the population of deer and other large
mammals, forcing natives to intensify their reliance on less succulent
resources such as acorns. Indian resource management techniques at the
time of the Gold Rush, however sustainable, thus represented centuries
of experience and practices resulting from a process of trial and error.[7]

The first Europeans reached California in September 1542, when
Juan Rodríguez Cabrillo, exploring the Pacific coast of North America for Spain, came to present-day San Diego. He eventually sailed as
far north as the current boundary of California and Oregon, yet few
colonists followed in his wake. While Spanish colonization surged into
other parts of the Americas—by 1750, Spain controlled an enormous
territory arcing from Florida through New Spain and Peru to Buenos
Aires—colonization of California lagged. Until the middle of the eigh-
teenth century, the geography of California remained a mystery to
Spanish colonial officials. What little they knew convinced them that
California was too remote, too expensive to settle, and unlikely to contain wealthy city-states like those of Mexico or Peru.[8]

It was not until 1769 that a Spanish-born Franciscan missionary,
Junípero Serra, made his way north from Baja California to establish
a mission at San Diego. By the time Serra died in 1784, he and his followers had founded nine missions in California; by 1800 there were
eighteen missions between San Diego and San Francisco. The promi-
nence of missions in California was unusual; everywhere else in Spanish
America, the influence of the Church was declining. During the eigh-
teenth century, Spanish monarchs undertook a series of moderniza-
tion efforts—known as the Bourbon reforms—that in many respects
undercut the influence of the Church.[9] In California, by contrast, the
missions were paramount. Because of the dominance of missionaries,
the Spanish colony in California assumed a very different character
from other eighteenth-century Spanish holdings in the Americas. It was,
in many respects, something of a backward-looking enterprise where
the missions dominated the economy and the culture. One consequence
of the missions' control over California was that settlement was halting;

the missions controlled most of the best land in the remote colony. Few colonists were tempted to settle there. The non-Indian population of California grew slowly, from 900 in 1790 to 1,800 in 1800 to 3,200 in 1821.

Spain's military presence in California was likewise thin. At San Diego and Monterey, the Spanish established two *presidios* (military posts), but the soldiers were occupied less with protecting California from Spain's imperial competitors (for most of its history, the province's remoteness and poverty was enough of a disincentive for potential rivals) than with helping the missionaries control the native population. The missions were the heart of the social order in California. With the help of soldiers, the missionaries gathered almost the entire native population of coastal California into the missions. The missionaries not only sought to convert the natives—they baptized tens of thousands—they also integrated them into the colony's economy. The missionaries controlled land, livestock, and labor. They instructed the baptized Indian neophytes in new skills: brickmaking, blacksmithing, farming, and herding. The Indians were essentially forced laborers. If they tried to leave the missions, soldiers would track them down and return them. If they disobeyed, they were punished with whippings, stocks, or irons. Soldiers at the presidios also commanded Indian labor. Their method differed from that of the missionaries: Spanish soldiers arrested Indians for various crimes—real or imagined—and sentenced them to convict labor, such as repairing the presidio buildings or serving in the presidio commander's household. This treatment prompted some Indian rebellions. In 1775, the Indians at the San Diego mission rebelled and killed a priest. There was violence at San Gabriel in 1785, San Diego (again) in 1786, San Luis Obispo in 1794, and Santa Barbara in 1824.[10]

During the mission period, the native population plummeted. Along the Pacific coast between San Diego and San Francisco, the Indian population fell from 72,000 to 18,000 over a half-century. Many Indians perished as a result of diseases such as smallpox and measles that the Spanish colonists had unwittingly introduced. Owing to the combination of disease and the harsh labor regime, an average Indian survived in a mission for only twelve years. Despite the threat of punishment if caught, large numbers of mission Indians ran away to the interior—every mission experienced a fugitivism rate of between 5 and 15 percent over the course of its existence. If the runaways could get a fair distance away from the missions, they were relatively safe: The Spaniards' control extended only about one day's march from the coast.[11]

Mexico's independence from Spain in 1821 spelled the end of the missions. In an effort to boost California's population and stimulate the economy, newly-independent Mexico undertook a series of land reforms. The 1824 Colonization Act, authorizing the Mexican government to grant large tracts of land to entrepreneurs, was followed in 1833 by the Secularization Act, according to which Mexico confiscated the lands of the missions. Between 1833 and 1846, the Mexican government made over 450 land grants—many of which were tens of thousands of acres in extent—to entrepreneurs who, it was hoped, would sponsor immigration. Yet California's economy remained sluggish. Unable to attract many settlers, those who received grants of land in California—a group largely comprised of Mexicans and other Latin Americans but that also included large numbers of Britons and Americans—employed Indians from the former missions to tend the thousands of cattle that had also once belonged to the missions. This rural elite—known as *rancheros* or *Californios*—sustained themselves selling cattle hide and tallow to British and American merchant vessels (Document 18).[12]

Many of the Californios had belonged to successful merchant families in Mexico or elsewhere in Spanish America. Following the usual path of upward mobility in Mexico, they plowed the profits of their commercial enterprises into large estates that drained their resources but conferred prestige. Juan Bandini, for instance, was born in Lima, Peru, the son of a successful Spanish merchant. A proponent of secularization and economic development, he received his first land grant—an estate near San Diego—in 1834. His future son-in-law was the Massachusetts-born merchant Abel Stearns, who went to sea as a twelve-year-old orphan, became a successful merchant in Mexico, and eventually controlled 450,000 acres in southern California. Bandini and Stearns—the latter listed his occupation as "gentleman" in the 1850 Census—both relished their aristocratic pretensions: they were "Don Juan" and "Don Abel." Every *vaquero*—the Indians who herded the cattle on the estates—bowed and doffed his cap when they passed by.[13] Their wealth and status plummeted after the gold rush as drought destroyed their cattle and the U.S. Land Commission challenged their property titles (Documents 20–22).

One of the most ambitious men to receive a grant in California was a failed rather than successful merchant, John Sutter, who was born Johann August Sutter in Germany of Swiss parents. In 1834, Sutter left Europe, his wife and five children, and an enormous debt from a failed dry-goods store. He abided a while in Missouri where he represented himself as a Prussian officer and former aide to the crown prince (he had, in fact, merely served in a local Swiss militia); he also worked as a trader, traveling widely to Santa Fe, Oregon, and Hawaii; and he received a 50,000-acre grant near present-day Sacramento in 1839. There, he set himself up as something of a seigneurial lord. He retained an honor guard of local natives. He built a fort (using imported workers from Hawaii) with adobe walls 18-feet high, which was to be the capital of what he called "New Helvetia" (Document 19).[14]

During this period, the United States had designs on California not because Americans had as yet any knowledge of the vast mineral wealth beneath California's surface, but for the strategic value of San Francisco Bay. In 1835, President Andrew Jackson offered to purchase San Francisco Bay and its surrounding territory from Mexico for $500,000 (he made a far more generous offer for Texas around the same time). President James Polk renewed the offer for northern California—raising the bid to $4 million—after assuming office in 1845. That offer became moot after Polk precipitated war with Mexico in 1846 over the southern boundary of the newly-annexed state of Texas. Around the same time, anticipating that war with Mexico would soon begin, an American officer in the Oregon country, John Frémont, joined with a handful of American migrants and embarked on a quixotic revolt against Mexican authority. His small force, the Bear Flaggers, so-called because of the standard they adopted, was soon brought under the command of the United States. When the United States acquired California from Mexico according to the Treaty of Guadalupe Hidalgo, which ended the United States–Mexico War in February 1848, American officials imagined nothing more than that they were acquiring the strategically significant harbor of San Francisco. The rest of California was, they believed, merely an unproductive and underpopulated province on Mexico's northwestern fringe. The province's non-Indian population was just 14,000. Its largest town, Los Angeles, had just 2,000 inhabitants. In February 1848, there was as yet no reason for anyone to believe that California would be, under American control, anything other than the remote, rural, underdeveloped, sparsely-populated province it had been under Mexico.

THE GOLD RUSH

The discovery of gold immediately changed American expectations for California. Before the discovery, California had been a sleepy province that struggled to attract immigrants and generate wealth. Within a year of annexation, tens of thousands of immigrants were contesting for control of California's riches. In addition to great wealth, the rapidity and scale of the Gold Rush produced chaotic social, political, and environmental disruptions. Miners improvised not only mining regulations, but the social order of camp life. They pushed Indians out of desired territories—often violently so. While white emigrants celebrated the Gold Rush for the possibility for upward mobility it offered them, they relegated Indians, Mexicans, Chileans, and immigrant Chinese workers to subordinate positions in the social hierarchy. Yet, for most miners, the promise of great wealth and upward mobility was illusory. Other wealth-seekers jostled to build what they hoped would be the capital city of the mining country; the pursuit meant fending off—again, often violently—land claimants and political rivals. In central California, prospectors and squatters pushed Mexican rancheros off of their lands.

The discovery of gold deposits in the foothills of the Sierra Nevada in California in early 1848—and just as importantly, the popularization of that discovery—changed not only the fate of California but of the United States. James Marshall, a carpenter building a sawmill for Sutter on the South Fork of the American River, discovered gold in the riverbed in January 1848. Despite the popular myth that word of the discovery spread instantaneously, Marshall, Sutter, and the few others who knew of the discovery—including the workmen constructing the sawmill—managed to keep the discovery secret for some time (Document 2). Word of the discovery did not appear in a California newspaper until mid-March. In that month, several former members of the Mormon Battalion—a hastily formed unit of volunteers who had joined the U.S. Army in the war against Mexico and ended up marching to California—began successfully sifting for gold on an island in the American River (Document 1). For most of 1848, news of the discovery remained localized to the Pacific: Most of the 20,000 people who arrived in California in 1848 in search of gold came from Hawaii and Mexico. It was not until President Polk included a report from Richard Mason, California's military governor, in his December 1848 annual message to Congress that Americans in the eastern United States became enthused about California gold (Document 3).

By the end of 1849, 100,000 people had migrated to California from the eastern United States, Latin America, Europe, and East Asia. Between 25,000 and 30,000 of those people were Americans who traveled overland to California in 1849. Despite popular notions that Plains Indians preyed on overland emigrants, of the half-million Americans who migrated across the Great Plains between 1840 and 1860, only 362 died at the hands of Indians—slightly fewer than the number of Indians killed by emigrants. Forty-niners had more to fear from cholera, which had broken out in the United States in 1848 to devastating effect: 10 percent of the population of St. Louis, Missouri, died of the disease in 1849. Cholera killed numerous emigrants and would-be emigrants on the first leg of their journey west. The disease, carried to California by emigrants, also made a brief but destructive appearance in Sacramento in 1850 (Document 10). Emigrants' own inexperience, and the dubious advice of guidebooks, was also a danger. The fate of the Donner party, who took an ill-advised shortcut to California in 1846, found themselves stranded in the Sierra Nevada in the winter of 1846–1847, and resorted to cannibalism to survive, was a sobering reminder of the dangers of overland travel. Wisely, perhaps, 40,000 Americans eschewed the overland route and chose to travel to California by sea. Many of these found that the fastest route to California was to take a ship from the eastern United States coast to Panama, cross the narrow isthmus, and then board another ship on the Pacific side for California.[15]

For many argonauts, California was not a permanent destination. So-called "go-backs," who turned around and returned east before completing the overland journey, comprised about 10 percent of overland emigrants. In 1850, 36,000 people arrived in San Francisco by sea, but another 26,000 departed. Over the course of the 1850s, departures were at least as high as 50 percent of arrivals. After a time in California, thousands of prospectors decamped for what were reputed to be even richer goldfields in Australia and British Columbia. Between 1852 and 1860, roughly 18,000 Americans joined the Gold Rush to Australia. Between 15,000 and 20,000 people left San Francisco for British Columbia in 1858 alone (Document 17). Such mobility typified nineteenth-century American migrants, who typically moved not once in their lives but several times.[16]

As the willingness of Forty-niners to leave California for Australia or British Columbia indicates, the California Gold Rush was a transnational phenomenon. Altogether about one-fourth of the migrants to California in the early years after the discovery of gold had been born outside of the United States. Perhaps 10,000 Mexicans migrated to California in 1848, and 5,000 Chileans by mid-1849 (Document 15). Two thousand men left Australia for California in the second half of 1849 (Document 16). Chinese migration to California peaked in 1852, when 20,000 migrants arrived. Historians once thought that famine and the violence of the Taiping Rebellion and Opium Wars drove the Chinese migration to California, but the majority of Chinese migrants to California came from the relatively prosperous, market-oriented, and outward-looking Pearl River delta. That region's trans-Pacific commercial ties drew migrants to California.[17] By contrast, famine drove the Irish to California. Only a small fraction of the hundreds of thousands who left Ireland as a result of the famine of the 1840s and early 1850s had enough money to travel as far as California, but 2,500 nonetheless had made it there by 1850. The failed liberal revolutions of 1848 in continental Europe drove thousands of German and French migrants to California. There were already 3,000 Germans in California by 1850. By 1853, there were 28,000 French citizens in California—more than in any official French colony. In 1849 Karl Marx rued how the French government distracted the urban poor from local conditions by holding out the promise of gold, writing that "the dreams of gold had replaced the dreams of socialism among the proletariat of Paris."[18]

As Marx understood, California suggested that workers equipped with nothing more than simple tools—pans, picks, and shovels—could reap immense wealth in return for their labor. Gold in California was found in what are called placer deposits. (Placer is a Spanish nautical term meaning "sandbank.") Placer deposits, in which some of the surrounding rock is eroded and nuggets, dust, or flakes of gold are found among gravel, are much easier to mine than lode deposits, in which the gold veins are encased in rock. Mason's 1848 report on the goldfields documented how gold-seekers used rudimentary tools: a shovel, a tin pan, and a rudely-constructed wooden cradle to sift gravel for gold flakes (Documents 2, 3, 15). These techniques were practiced best by those Americans who had searched for gold in Georgia in the 1830s and, in far greater numbers, by Sonorans who had worked in mines in Mexico's Sierra Madre. Their practices quickly diffused among less—experienced gold-seekers. For the first few prospectors to reach the gold country, panning for gold could be rewarding. After spring floods had receded, the clear streams that flowed out of the Sierra Nevada became a relative trickle, and some gold flakes and nuggets were visible to the naked eye in the pebbly stream bottoms. In 1849 and 1850, many prospectors could glean an ounce of gold a day from their claims.[19]

Yet, as Mason's account makes clear, prospectors did not work alone. Mason noted that it took four men to operate the cradle: one to shovel gravel from the bank, another to empty it into the cradle, a third to keep the apparatus rocking, and a fourth to keep water flowing through it. Success in extracting gold from California's streams thus depended not on individual labor but on cooperation. Teams of miners formed themselves into companies that undertook increasingly elaborate operations: building dams to expose gravel on the bed of streams and diverting water into long sluice boxes—the cradles being too small to handle the ever larger amounts of gravel miners sought to process (Document 5). As the gold country became crowded with prospectors, miners had to improvise rules to prevent conflict among themselves—rules that initially were merely custom and not law. In 1848, only about 5,000 miners populated the streambanks in the Sierra Nevada foothills; there was still plenty of room for everyone. By the next year, however, the number of miners had swarmed to 40,000. In order to prevent collisions, miners staked claims to the area they worked. In 1849, riverbank prospectors could stake out claims to the minerals below the earth without holding title to the land; most of the land in question belonged to the federal government. These claims were bounded, of course, by certain restrictions. Prospectors' claims were limited in both extent and number (usually no more than one). If unworked, a prospector's claim lapsed entirely. Those claims varied in size: in late 1848, Peter Burnett, later governor of California, was one of a group of partners who laid claim to 1,000 square feet, including 20 feet of frontage along the Yuba River. By mid-1850, claims were as small as 15 square feet. The amount of land or river frontage one could claim varied by locality, but generally, after recording a claim with a local clerk, the custom was for miners to retain their right to their claim by working it regularly and, when not present, to leave their tools on the site. The regulations thus both drew upon and supported the mid-nineteenth-century notion of free labor: each prospector was entitled to a single claim of limited extent so long as he labored at it.[20] No rules could ensure success at the mines, however: Most prospectors failed (Documents 4, 6, 11).

The free-labor system of mining gold was not the only labor regime in California in the 1850s. Because effective placer mining required teams of laborers, numerous Southern slaveholders brought their slaves with them to California to mine for gold. California lawmakers wanted neither slavery nor free blacks in the new state. At the California Constitutional Convention in 1849, legislators unanimously voted to petition for admission to the Union as a free state. At the same time, they endorsed the idea of forbidding free blacks from residing in the state (Document 13). However, even after California's admission as a free state in 1850, slavery persisted. By 1852, there were 2,000 African Americans in California, roughly half of whom were slaves. In 1857, the California legislature revisited the idea of barring free blacks from the state, prompting large numbers of African Americans to join the exodus to the new gold fields in British Columbia. At the same time, some slaves successfully petitioned for their freedom in California before they could be returned to the South (Document 14).[21]

However much white miners cooperated among themselves to create an orderly and efficient system for claiming and working gold deposits, in numerous other respects conflict and violence characterized Gold Rush California. Spanish/Mexican settlement had hugged the Pacific coast; Sutter's outpost near the juncture of the Sacramento and American rivers was an outlier. Indians in the foothills of the Sierra Nevada—the heart of the gold country—had thus remained relatively autonomous from the missions and the ranchos that succeeded them. When miners first entered the gold country, the Indians vastly outnumbered them. Desperate for laborers, many of the earliest miners employed Indians to sift gravel for gold. In 1848, Mason encountered one such miner, John Sinclair, with fifty Indians in his employ on the North Fork of the American River. At the southern end of the gold country, where the Indians had longer experience with Euroamericans, such relatively peaceful economic relationships were common. As one moved north, however, violence typified miner-Indian encounters. Both miners and Indians sought to control the river valleys, and the uses to which they put the rivers were exclusive: Indians needed the streams for salmon, miners for gold. Miners' dams and diversions effectively ruined the rivers for salmon. Conflict resulted. Over the course of the 1850s, companies of miners killed thousands of Indians, destroying entire villages and massacring their inhabitants in response to real or alleged Indian violence (Documents 23–26).[22]

American prospectors also resorted to violence against Spanish-speaking miners to expel them from rich claims or extort from them their wealth. On the Calaveras River in 1849, a group of vigilante American miners rounded up a group of one hundred Mexicans; a self-appointed judge fined each of the Mexicans an ounce of gold, which was divided among the vigilantes as recompense for their troubles. This sort of extortion masquerading as law could be deadly. Later in 1849, for instance, vigilantes apprehended sixteen Chilean miners and charged them with murder. A tribunal of American miners found the Chileans guilty; all of them were executed. The Californians' system of justice in the mining camps was thus one that was limited to white Anglo miners; others could not expect that the protections of the system would be extended to them.[23]

Gold-seekers swarmed over the landholdings of the Californios. Prospectors trampled Sutter's wheat and scattered his livestock. Miners were followed by settlers, many of whom had no intention of respecting the rancheros' titles to the lands under Mexican law. The settlers asserted that the Mexican land grants were void, invoked their right to stake a claim to United States public land, and simply squatted on the rancheros' lands. Some rancheros struck a deal with squatters by negotiating sharecropping or tenant contracts with them. For most rancheros, however, squatters were a nuisance.[24] A still greater threat to the Californios' lands was the United States Land Commission, established in 1851 to investigate the legitimacy of land grants made by the Mexican government. The Land Commission investigated 813 land grants. The commissioners ultimately confirmed 75 percent of the grants, but in many cases they reduced the size of the estates. For some rancheros, the expense of fighting for their land grants in court—a process that in some cases extended for years—was ruinous (Document 20).[25]

Socially, one of the unusual characteristics of 1850s California was that it was overwhelmingly male. Roughly 90 percent of the people who traveled to California in 1848 and 1849 were men. In 1860, the California population was still 66 percent male. As in other places in the nineteenth-century West dominated by male labor, such as logging camps, ranches, and Army outposts, prostitution in Gold Rush California was highly visible. The skewed gender ratio also conferred a certain leverage on some women, however. The relative scarcity of women encouraged a public sentiment toward permitting unhappily married women to divorce; California courts liberalized divorce rules to the point that mid-century California women sought divorces at a much higher rate than other Americans.[26]

By 1860, the California population had reached 400,000. The majority of emigrants to California settled not in the gold country but in one of the many cities that arose as commercial centers for the mining country. San Francisco grew from fewer than 1,000 inhabitants in 1848 to over 50,000 by 1860, by which time it had become the fifteenth-largest city in the United States. (For comparison's sake, it had taken New York City almost two hundred years to reach a population of 50,000.) Sacramento, the primary nexus of commerce for the gold country, had a population of 2,000 in 1849, over 9,000 in 1850, and over 24,000 in 1860. Not all cities thrived: the town of Vernon, for instance, started with great fanfare but folded after a year (Document 7). Vernon notwithstanding, the California Gold Rush spurred immense urban growth. The rapid rise of cities occurred in part because, like the mines, many of the cities—especially those in the gold country—themselves were speculative enterprises, founded by groups of local merchants who anticipated fortunes in real estate. Sacramento's city government in the early 1850s, for instance, was dominated by the men who owned city lots; the municipal government was a kind of board of directors for these investors in city real estate. In August 1850, a simmering conflict between the city govern-ment and settlers who challenged the legality of the investors' property titles boiled over into violence. On August 14, a dozen squatters and sev-eral city officials, including the sheriff and the city assessor, were killed in a day of pitched battles in the city. The governor ordered the state militia to restore order, and the city government managed to establish its authority, if not its legitimacy (Documents 8, 9).[27]

San Francisco was likewise beset by spasms of lawlessness and vigi-lante violence in the 1850s. In 1849, merchants hired a private security force to police the waterfront. Many of the recruits to this private police force were members of a gang of thugs, the "Sydney Ducks," from the penal colony of Australia. The gang, whose members took to calling themselves the "Hounds" in San Francisco, preyed on vulnerable inhab-itants of the city until a vigilante committee of 200 men rounded them up and deported them in 1851. Five years later, a much larger vigilante committee assumed effective control over the city. They came to power in early 1856, when one of the leaders of the 1851 vigilantes reorga-nized his followers and lynched two accused murderers. Over the next months, the vigilantes harassed and deported dozens and hanged two more accused murderers. In August, 6,000 vigilantes marched in a vic-tory parade through the city in celebration of their purported estab-lishment of order, before officially disbanding (Document 12). Yet the vigilantes' political wing, the People's Party, continued to rule San Francisco through, as one historian put it, the vigilantes' paradoxical combination of "blood, propaganda, and respectability."[28]

Chinese immigrants to California escaped the wrath of the vigilantes in San Francisco in 1856, but were in other respects subject to routine discrimination and spasms of deadly violence. The number of Chinese in California went from almost none when gold was first discovered to 25,000 in 1852—or 10 percent of the population of the state. Like many European immigrants who arrived on the Atlantic coast of the United States, many Chinese immigrants intended to abide in Califor-nia only briefly before returning home having amassed some savings. Accordingly, like the Anglo migrants to California, the Chinese were overwhelmingly young and male. As late as 1870, only one out of every thirteen Chinese immigrants in California was a woman. Altogether, between 1848 and 1880, roughly 322,000 Chinese arrived in the United States and 151,000 left. Chinese miners often worked claims that other miners had abandoned—and they did so successfully. Anglo miners' resentment against the Chinese was even more pronounced than their disregard for Latin American prospectors. In 1850, the California state legislature imposed a $20 monthly tax on foreign miners—a law that fell primarily on Chinese miners. Armed white miners routinely expelled Chinese miners from their claims (Documents 27–30).[29]

In all, battles over authority and legitimacy characterized California in the first years after the discovery of gold. Whiteness and property informed many Californians' sense of legitimacy. While white prospectors were able to sort out a peaceable system for claims in the mining camps, in other respects California's social and political environment was chaotic. White miners violently asserted their belief that non-whites' rights to mine for gold—or, in the case of Indians or African Americans, even to inhabit the gold country—were not equal to their own. Settlers challenged property titles that were based on Mexican land grants. City governments established their authority through the use or threat of violence. In an environment of chaos, the privileged and the powerful prevailed.

AFTER THE GOLD RUSH

Between 1849 and 1858, California produced over $550 million in gold—over $10 billion in current value. The Gold Rush accelerated American westward expansion: the transcontinental railroad, completed in 1869, linked Sacramento to the eastern United States. The infusion of bullion into the American economy fueled the United States' mid-nineteenth-century industrial takeoff. Fundamentally, the wealth that the Gold Rush created came from a massive alteration to the California environment (Documents 31, 32). The extraction of minerals from the ground had significant environmental consequences. By the end of the 1850s, pollution from mining debris had already become an unavoidable problem (Document 36). In southern California, the rancheros joined the scramble for wealth, hoping to become rich by supplying beef to the gold country—until overstocking of the range and drought combined to dash their plans (Document 21).

In many ways, California in the years immediately after the Gold Rush was an emerging industrial place. The state produced almost one billion dollars in gold between 1849 and 1874. Though most of that wealth was exported from California, enough of it remained to spur other industry in the state; California manufacturing, excluding gold mining, rose from a value of under $4 million in 1850 to $116 million in 1880. California's rapid industrialization exemplified the startling industrial growth of the nation. The United States' relative share of world manufacturing output rose from a mere 7 percent in 1860 (when it ranked behind Britain,

France, China, and India), to 14 percent in 1880 (when it was second only to Britain), to 24 percent in 1900 (when it was the world leader).

Like all industrializing nations, the United States achieved its economic growth in the nineteenth century through the combined exploitation of what economists call the three "factors of production": capital, labor, and natural resources. Remarkably, the nineteenth-century United States was chronically short of the first two of these three ingredients of industrial growth, capital and labor. At great cost, the United States imported a significant proportion of its capital and labor from abroad. At the end of the nineteenth century approximately one-third of American investment capital came from Europe and one-fifth of American wage-earners were immigrants. In Gold Rush California, where 25 percent of argonauts had been born outside the United States, the percentage of foreign-born workers was even higher. Moreover, California laborers were unruly, transient, and, most importantly, expensive. Investment capital was scarce in California, too: Of the nearly $525 million invested in manufacturing in the United States in 1850, only a little over $1 million was invested in California. In 1854 much of the California economy operated on credit, and in early 1855 several California banks closed. Investment capital was so hard to find in Gold Rush California that some mining companies offered clerical positions in return for loans.[30] Almost all of the bullion produced in California was exported out of the state, so despite producing roughly one-third of the world's gold in the 1850s, California was chronically short of capital.

While capital and labor were scarce and expensive, natural resources were abundant. Law and technology worked in concert in Gold Rush California to shift the burden of industrialization to the exploitation of natural resources. State and federal authorities enacted legislation that liberalized access to mineral resources. In California and elsewhere in the West, state and federal courts facilitated the transfer of natural resources in the public domain to the control of private industrialists through a series of friendly rulings. Precisely because industrialization relied disproportionately on cheap natural resources, it exacted heavy environmental costs.

By the mid-1850s, labor-intensive means of exploiting gold deposits such as pans and cradles had given way to the industrial techniques of hydraulic mining (Document 33). Mining was seasonal work. High water in the spring prevented miners from working the streambeds. Low riverflow in the summer made it difficult to wash gravel for gold. The unpredictability of the riverine environment impeded the search for gold. To regularize the flow of water, miners constructed reservoirs.

Impounding water was a necessary precondition for the development of the single most important technology in the exploitation of placer deposits: the machinery of hydraulic mining. As early as 1852, engineers used pressurized water from a reservoir to flush gravel into a sluice. Eventually, as engineers perfected the technology, they were able to make water shoot out of the hoses at speeds up to 100 miles per hour. The force of the water carved large craters out of the Sierra foothills. High-pressure water cannons washed hillsides into sluices—effectively larger versions of the prospectors' cradles—constructed to trap gold but let soil and gravel wash away. The sluices flushed these tailings into the streams that flowed out of the Sierra.

A series of California Supreme Court decisions in the 1850s established hydraulic miners' right to divert streams and deposit debris in riverways. In an October 1855 case, *Tarter* v. *Spring Creek Water and Mining Company*, the California Supreme Court ruled that hydraulic mining companies enjoyed a "*quasi* private proprietorship" to the use of rivers. In several cases, California jurists eroded the ability of lawyers to categorize hydraulic miners' ditches, which frequently overflowed and flooded neighbors' lands, as nuisances. The transformation of the California legal environment paralleled the economic transformation of the state: from independent, technologically rudimentary prospectors to technologically sophisticated industries.

Hydraulic mining exacted startling environmental costs. By the mid-1860s, debris from hydraulic gold mining had fouled and flooded rivers that drained into the Sacramento River, and ultimately into San Francisco Bay, destroying both fish and farmland. By one estimate, between the mid-1850s and the early 1880s, hydraulic mining deposited 885 million cubic yards of debris in California rivers—over three times the amount of earth moved to make way for the Panama Canal. Mining sediment discolored the water of San Francisco Bay so extensively that in the 1870s it was visible in the Golden Gate. Moreover, hydraulic miners used mercury, a toxic mineral mined and processed near San Jose, as an amalgam in their sluices (Document 34). Large amounts of mercury also found its way into the river environment. Debris piled so high in the Bear and Yuba rivers that all but the tops of pine trees on the banks were submerged. Downstream, debris filled river channels; the channel of the Yuba was filled so completely that by the 1870s the stream ran a mile away from its original course. Debris spoiled salmon spawning grounds: In 1878, the Commissioners of Fisheries reported that hydraulic mining debris had destroyed half of the salmon habitat in the state.

Debris raised riverbeds, causing spring floods to inundate farmlands with a watery mixture of sand and gravel that farmers dubbed "slickens." The mixture was poisonous to humans, other animals, and soil. In order to confine the waters of the spring floods, farmers raised levees. As new deposits of sediment accreted on the riverbeds, they raised the levees further. By 1878, stretches of the Bear River's bed were actually higher than the surrounding countryside. Towns along the rivers also had to build levees to prevent against the floods. In 1875, the flood broke through the levee at Marysville and inundated the town. In 1878, floods covered the entire lower Sacramento valley, leaving Marysville and Sacramento as islands behind their levees. In short, industrial mining did not extract wealth from the non-human natural environment so much as it rearranged the distribution of natural wealth: benefiting hydraulic mining companies to the detriment of farms, cities, and fisheries.

Environmental change was not limited to mining. Californians cut great numbers of trees for ore reduction, shaft timbers, and the construction of the rapidly expanding towns of Sacramento, San Francisco, Marysville, and Stockton. By the end of the 1860s, approximately one-third of the state's timber had been cut. California ranchers initially reaped profits in the 1850s when they shifted from selling hides and tallow to passing Yankee merchant ships to driving their cattle north to the gold country. Like ranchers elsewhere in the North American West in the nineteenth century, they found the temptation to put more cattle on the range in the hope of reaping profits too great to resist. Yet heavy winter rains in late 1861, followed by drought in 1863–1864, caused the California cattle ranching industry to collapse. There were some three million horses, cattle, and sheep in California on the eve of the drought; by the time it was over some 800,000 had died.

In short, in the 1860s and 1870s, Californians began to reckon with the environmental consequences of a mining economy. They had exploited minerals, trees, and grasslands extensively and wastefully. California's resource-intensive economy, in which capital and labor were scarce and expensive, had dictated that strategy. As the economy diversified, however, farmers and city-dwellers in the Sacramento Valley began to oppose the hydraulic mines and their owners' assertions that floods and pollution were an unavoidable necessity of modern industrial life. They were joined in their opposition by one of the most powerful corporations in California, the Southern Pacific Railroad. By the 1870s, the Southern Pacific's directors had decided that California's future was not in mining but in agriculture. The company bankrolled the legal challenge to hydraulic mining, which ended with a federal judge's permanent injunction against the practice in 1884 in *Woodruff* v. *North Bloomfield Hydraulic Mining Company* (Documents 35–37). Hydraulic mining companies took their technologies elsewhere, such as British Columbia, where hydraulic mining remained legal. In California, they sold the water from the reservoirs they controlled to cities and Central Valley farmers. Indeed, much of the water for California's irrigated agriculture sector came, initially, from reservoirs initially constructed for hydraulic mining.[31]

THE GOLD RUSH IN HISTORICAL MEMORY

Despite the vast and sudden social, political, and environmental changes the Gold Rush wrought, in popular memory the Gold Rush is remembered—more than a little romantically—as an entrepreneurial adventure: rather like a busy day at the stock exchange after which all the traders went home tired but happy and much, much richer. The iconography of the Gold Rush, in works by the artists Charles Christian Nahl and August Wenderoth among others, reduced non-white Californians to entertaining diversions, erased the environmental damage caused by technologies such as hydraulic mining, and promoted (as a symbol of the virtues of free labor and upward mobility) the image of the lone prospector using simple tools to pan for gold by a stream.

For over 150 years, the icon of the California Gold Rush has been that prospector, a symbol of upward social mobility. Abraham Lincoln summed up the ideology undergirding that symbol in a speech in 1859: "The prudent, penniless beginner in the world, labors for wages awhile, saves a surplus with which to buy tools or land, for himself; then labors on his own account another while, and at length hires another new beginner to help him." For mid-nineteenth-century Americans, the West was where they believed upward social mobility was most possible.

By the 1880s, writers such as Josiah Royce, Charles Shinn, and Hubert Howe Bancroft (Documents 38–40) extended upon those ideas to memorialize the Gold Rush as an economic windfall while celebrating the first generation of Californians for having engineered what they saw as a smooth transition from a collection of mining camps to a prosperous and democratic state.

The California Gold Rush generally remains thus understood within American history: as a celebration of western settlement and of free labor. It is an understanding that is romanticized and sanitized. In many United States history textbooks, the romance of the Gold Rush serves as comic relief in the grim run-up to the Civil War—a triumphal story of new wealth found and new territory settled in the midst of the declensionist narrative of sectionalism and the descent into civil war. So, too, is the history sanitized. Despite recent work by historians documenting white miners' violence against Indians, Latin Americans, and Chinese, in popular understanding that violence is largely erased. Similarly, by the end of the 1850s, the pans and shovels of the prospectors had given way to the industrial techniques of hydraulic mining. Most of the miners who remained in the gold country were not independent prospectors but wage earners in the hydraulic mines. The persistence of the icon of the prospector—alone and in small groups, using simple tools—overwhelms the historical reality of industrial mining and its pollution. Nahl and Wenderoth, for instance, went on producing canvases extolling the prospector into the 1870s even though that era had long before vanished.

When understood in historical context, the California Gold Rush seems less like the romantic adventure it is popularly remembered to be. The Gold Rush was part of nineteenth-century American western conquest: The United States acquired California from Mexico just as gold was discovered; asserted its authority over the territory at the expense of many Mexican landholders; and offered to California's natives a devil's bargain: die, or be amalgamated into the new order as a racialized working class. While the Gold Rush in California was a story of U.S. expansion, it was also part of a circum-Pacific world of gold rushes and transnational movements of people. Many Americans reached California not overland but by sea, joining the Chileans, Australians, Chinese, and others who sailed to California. And many of those who journeyed to California in the first years after the discovery of gold left just as quickly, first for the gold fields of Australia and then for those in British Columbia. Thousands of argonauts professed, through their movements, a loyalty not to any nation but to gold, wherever it might be found. In this respect, they were not unlike the secessionists in the southern states, who professed a loyalty to their property in slaves over their U.S. citizenship. For white argonauts like white Southerners, race more than nation commanded their loyalty: White argonauts in California did not hesitate to exclude, threaten, deport, or even murder non-white competitors to their search for wealth. Nor did miners hesitate to cause significant damage to the environment in their search for gold. In short, miners sacrificed much on the altar of gold. What James Beith, a Scottish immigrant to California, wrote of American argonauts in 1857 could well apply to all of the gold-seekers in California: "If the Gates of Hell were hinged with Gold, a Yankee would go there and take them."

NOTES

[1]Thomas Richards, Jr., "'Farewell to America': The Expatriation Politics of Overland Migration, 1841–1846," *Pacific Historical Review* 86 (February 2017): 114–52.

[2]Kenneth N. Owens, *California Mormons and the Great Rush for Riches* (Norman: University of Oklahoma Press, 2004).

[3]Leonard L. Richards, *The California Gold Rush and the Coming of the Civil War* (New York: Knopf, 2007).

[4]Andrea G. McDowell, "From Commons to Claims: Property Rights in the California Gold Rush," *Yale Journal of Law and the Humanities* 14 (2002): 1–72.

[5]See, for instance, James J. Rawls, *Indians of California: The Changing Image* (Norman: University of Oklahoma Press, 1984), 19; Albert L. Hurtado, *Indian Survival on the California Frontier* (New Haven: Yale University Press, 1988), 135; Brendan Lindsay, *Murder State: California's Native American Genocide, 1846–1873* (Lincoln: University of Nebraska Press, 2012); Benjamin Madley, *An American Genocide: The United States and the California Indian Catastrophe, 1846–1873* (New Haven: Yale University Press, 2016).

[6]See M. Kat Anderson, Michael G. Barbour, and Valerie Whitworth, "A World of Balance and Plenty: Land, Plants, Animals, and Humans in a Pre-European California," in *Contested Eden: California Before the Gold Rush*, eds. Ramón A. Gutiérrez and Richard Orsi (Berkeley: University of California Press, 1998), 12–47.

[7]See L. Mark Raab, "Political Ecology of Prehistoric Los Angeles," in *Land of Sunshine: An Environmental History of Metropolitan Los Angeles*, eds. William Deverell and Greg Hise (Pittsburgh: University of Pittsburgh Press, 2005), 23–37. For the environmental history of California, see Arthur F. McEvoy, Jr., *The Fisherman's Problem: Ecology and Law in the California Fisheries, 1850–1980* (New York: Cambridge University Press, 1986); Andrew C. Isenberg, *Mining California: An Ecological History* (New York: Hill and Wang, 2005).

[8]David J. Weber, *The Spanish Frontier in North America* (New Haven: Yale University Press, 1994); Paul W. Mapp, *The Elusive West and the Contest for Empire, 1713–1763* (Chapel Hill: University of North Carolina Press, 2011), 33–34.

[9]D. A. Brading, *Miners and Merchants in Bourbon Mexico, 1763–1810* (Cambridge: Cambridge University Press, 1971).

[10]Steven W. Hackel, *Children of Coyote, Missionaries of Saint Francis: Indian-Spanish Relations in Colonial California, 1769–1850* (Chapel Hill: University of North Carolina Press, 2005); Albert L. Hurtado, *Intimate Frontiers: Sex, Gender, and Culture in Old California* (Albuquerque: University of New Mexico Press, 1999), 1–19.

[11]Hurtado, *Indian Survival on the California Frontier*, 20–31.

[12]Steven W. Hackel, "Land, Labor, and Production: The Colonial Economy of Spanish and Mexican California," in *Contested Eden*, eds. Gutiérrez and Orsi, 111–46.

[13]Isenberg, *Mining California*, 110–17.

[14]Albert L. Hurtado, *John Sutter: A Life on the North American Frontier* (Norman: University of Oklahoma Press, 2006).

[15]John D. Unruh, Jr., *The Plains Across: The Overland Emigrants and the Trans-Mississippi West, 1840–60* (Urbana: University of Illinois Press, 1979); Aims McGuinness, *Path of Empire: Panama and the California Gold Rush* (Ithaca: Cornell University Press, 2008).

[16]Rodman W. Paul, "'Old Californians' in British Gold Fields," *Huntington Library Quarterly* 17 (February 1954): 161–72; Kenneth N. Owens. ed., *Riches for All: The California Gold Rush and the World* (Lincoln: University of Nebraska Press, 2002).

[17]Yong Chen, "The Internal Origins of Chinese Emigration to California Reconsidered," *Western Historical Quarterly* 28 (Winter 1997): 520–46.

[18]Malcolm J. Rohrbough, "'We Will Make Our Fortunes—No Doubt of It': The Worldwide Rush to California," in *Riches for All*, ed., Owens, 55–70.

[19]Isenberg, *Mining California*, 25–28.

[20]Malcolm J. Rohrbough, *Days of Gold: The California Gold Rush and the American Nation* (Berkeley: University of California Press, 1999).

[21]Rudolph M. Lapp, *Blacks in Gold Rush California* (New Haven: Yale University Press, 1977), 49–50, 134, 239–40; Stacey L. Smith, *Freedom's Frontier: California and the Struggle over Unfree Labor, Emancipation, and Reconstruction* (Chapel Hill: University of North Carolina Press, 2013).

[22]Hurtado, *Indian Survival on the California Frontier*, 100–24.

[23]Rohrbough, *Days of Gold*, 222–26.

[24]Albert Camarillo, *Chicanos in a Changing Society: From Mexican Pueblos to American Barrios in Santa Barbara and Southern California, 1848–1930* (Cambridge, MA: Harvard University Press, 1979), 114.

[25]Isenberg, *Mining California*, 103–30.

[26]Hurtado, *Intimate Frontiers*, 99–103.

[27]Donald Pisani, "Squatter Law in California, 1850–1858," *Western Historical Quarterly* 25 (Autumn 1994): 277–310.

[28]Philip J. Ethington, *The Public City: The Political Construction of Urban Life in San Francisco, 1850–1900* (New York: Cambridge University Press, 1994), 128.

[29]Alexander Saxton, *The Indispensable Enemy: Labor and the Anti-Chinese Movement in California* (Berkeley: University of California Press, 1971); Mae M. Ngai, "Chinese Gold Miners and the 'Chinese Question' in Nineteenth-Century California and Victoria," *Journal of American History* 101 (March 2015): 44–70.

[30]F. Halsey Rogers, "'Man to Loan $1500 and Serve as Clerk': Trading Jobs for Loans in Mid-Nineteenth-Century San Francisco," *Journal of Economic History* 54 (March 1994): 34–63.

[31]Isenberg, *Mining California*, 12–15, 23–51, 76–77, 121–30, 163–76.

PART TWO

The Documents

1

Discovery

James Marshall's discovery of gold on the South Fork of the American River set off a cascade of discoveries, as prospectors fanned out into the foothills of the Sierra Nevada. William T. Sherman, then an Army lieutenant posted to California at the end of the Mexican-American War, provided a detailed description of the discovery of gold and the early stages of the Gold Rush. So too did Sherman's commanding officer, Richard Mason, the military governor of California at the time of Marshall's discovery. It was Mason's report, appended to President James Polk's annual message to Congress in December 1848, that popularized the discovery of gold in the eastern United States. Sherman and Mason—observers of the prospectors rather than participants in the scramble for gold—gave an impression of panning for gold that made it seem facile, and the life of a prospector a kind of romantic adventure. For some of the earliest prospectors such as Azariah Smith, gold was easy to find. Yet panning for gold, or washing gold-bearing gravel through "rockers" or "long toms" was not effortless, especially for later-arriving miners. Joseph Pownall's 1850 letter described the difficulty of extracting gold from riverbeds. Joseph Chaffee described shortages of water and investment capital, among other challenges that faced gold miners. Eventually, they all made a discovery of their own: that the vast majority of men who came to the gold country failed to find a fortune. "Dame Shirley" (the pen name of Louise Amelia Knapp Smith Clapp, who accompanied her husband to the gold country in 1851 and 1852) understood the unpredictability of prospecting better than most. As she wrote, the entire effort was nothing but a gamble.

1

AZARIAH SMITH

The Gold Discovery Journal

1848

---

*Smith was eleven years old when his parents joined the Church of Latter
Day Saints in Ohio. In 1846, he was in Council Bluffs, Iowa, preparing
with his family and other Mormons to migrate to the Far West, when
instead, at the urging of church leaders, he volunteered for the Mormon
Battalion. The unit, comprised of just over 500 Mormon men and boys
(Smith himself was not yet 18 when he enlisted), served under General
Stephen Kearny during the U.S. war with Mexico. The Battalion
marched from Iowa to New Mexico to southern California, where they
were mustered out of service in the summer of 1847. From there, Smith
made his way north to the Sacramento Valley, where he found work and
looked forward to rejoining the Mormons in Utah. Smith was one of the
laborers constructing the sawmill under the direction of James Marshall
when Marshall spotted gold in the American River in early 1848.
Smith collected gold both at the site where Marshall discovered it, and
at Mormon Island in the American River, where two church members,
Sidney Willis and Wilford Hudson, found gold in March 1848.*

Sunday Jan. the 30th 48

Mr. Marshall haveing arived we got liberty of him, and built a small
house down by the mill, and last Sunday we moved into it in order to get
rid of the brawling, partial, mistress, and cook for ourselves. This week
Mon. the 24th. [date inserted later] Mr. Marshall found some pieces of
(as we all suppose) Gold, and he has gone to the Fort, for the Purpose
of finding out.

It is found in the raceway in small pieces; some have been found that
would weigh five dollars.

The Gold Discovery Journal of Azariah Smith, ed. David L. Bigler (Logan, UT: Utah State
University Press, 1998), 108–16.

Sunday Febuary the 6th

Mr. Marshall has returned with the fact that it is Gold; and Captain Sutter came here Wednesday ... for the purpose of looking at the mine, where the Gold is found, and got enough for a ring. The captain brought us a bottle of Liquor, and some pocket knives. ...

Monday Feb. the 14th

The past week I did not work but three days and a half. Mr. Marshall grants us the privelege of picking up Gold odd spells and Sundays, and I have gathered up considerable. When we shut down the gates the gold is found in the bottom of the tale race.

Sunday Feb. the 20th

The fore part of the past week it rained and I did not work but four days, and I have been drilling a rock which is in the race, and blasting, which pleases the Indians very much to see the rock which is very hard, split open so easy. Today I picked up a little more of the root of all evil.

Sunday March the 12th

The past two weeks, as usial, I have been to work on the mill; and last Sunday I picked up two dollars and a half, below this place about two miles. ...

Friday April the 7th

I have worked four days this week, but today I am laying by. Brot[hers] Brown, Stephens, and Bigler started today for the Fort, but I thought that I would stay and work. Mr. Marshall has gave us the privelige [of] hunting Gold and haveing half we find, and we are a going [to take] the opportunity. I have something like thirty dollars of [gold].

Saturday April the 15th

The Boys have returned [from the] Fort and brought word that the first company are to start for Salt Lake today, and the rest are to start on the first day of June, and I think that I Shall go down to the Fort and prepare for the trip. As I have worked out one hundred dollars and upwards, besides what Gold I have picked up, I think that I shall be able to fit myself out, if I can get my pay, in things that I want, and at a reasonable price. ...

Friday May the 26th

I scraped one day on the race, when on the nineth the boys came back from the exploring expedition haveing went up to the back bones which was covered with Snow and they could not cross. They then concluded to go up to the Gold mine, so on Thursday the 11th. we went up, and stayed there untill Tuesday the 23d., when we came down. While there we had very good luck; I got there something near three hundred dollars, which makes me in all some upwards of four hundred dollars. The most I made in a day was sixty five dollars after the toll was taken out, which was thirty dollars out of a hundred, which goes to Hudson and Willis, that discovered the mine, and Brannon[1] who is securing it for them. Before we came away, men, women and children, from the Bay and other places in California, were flocking to the gold mine, by the dozens, and by wagon loads. While there Brannon called a me[e]ting, to see who was willing to pay toll and who was not. The most of them agreed to pay toll, but some of them would not. ... Some of the boys came here last night that have been get[t]ing Gold on the other side of the river.

2

GENERAL WILLIAM T. SHERMAN

Memoirs

1875

William T. Sherman, born in Lancaster, Ohio, in 1820, entered West Point at age 16 on the recommendation of his foster father, U.S. Senator Thomas Ewing. He was commissioned as a second lieutenant in 1840 and saw action in the Second Seminole War in Florida. Sherman later became a celebrated general during the American Civil War, but his service during the Mexican-American War between 1846 and 1848 was limited to administrative duties in California. He spent seven months sailing for California, arriving in early 1847, by which time the province was effectively under American control. As an aide to the military governor, Colonel Richard Mason, he was one of the first Americans to become aware of James Marshall's discovery of gold in early 1848.

I remember one day, in the spring of 1848, that two men, Americans, came into the office and inquired for the Governor. I asked their business, and

[1]Sam Brannan, a successful publisher, merchant, and real estate speculator, was the leader of the Mormons in California until his fellowship was revoked in 1851.

The Memoirs of General William T. Sherman, vol 1. (New York: D. Appleton and Co., 1875), 40–54.

one answered that they had just come down from Captain Sutter on special business, and they wanted to see Governor Mason in person. I took them in to the colonel, and left them together. After some time the colonel came to his door and called to me. I went in, and my attention was directed to a series of papers unfolded on his table, in which lay about half an ounce of placer gold. Mason said to me, "What is that?" I touched it and examined one or two of the larger pieces, and asked, "Is it gold?" Mason asked me if I had ever seen native gold. I answered that, in 1844, I was in Upper Georgia, and there saw some native gold, but it was much finer than this, and that it was in phials, or in transparent quills; but I said that, if this were gold, it could be easily tested, first, by its malleability, and next by acids. I took a piece in my teeth, and the metallic lustre was perfect. I then called to the clerk, Baden, to bring an axe and hatchet from the backyard. When these were brought, I took the largest piece and beat it out flat, and beyond doubt it was metal, and a pure metal. Still, we attached little importance to the fact, for gold was known to exist at San Fernando, at the south, and yet was not considered of much value. Colonel Mason then handed me a letter from Captain Sutter, addressed to him, stating that he (Sutter) was engaged in erecting a saw-mill at Coloma, about forty miles up the American Fork, above his fort at New Helvetia, for the general benefit of the settlers in that vicinity; that he had incurred considerable expense, and wanted a "preemption" to the quarter-section of land on which the mill was located, embracing the tail-race in which this particular gold had been found. Mason instructed me to prepare a letter, in answer, for his signature. I wrote off a letter, reciting that California was yet a Mexican province, simply held by us as a conquest; that no laws of the United States yet applied to it, much less the land laws or preemption laws, which could only apply after a public survey. Therefore it was impossible for the Governor to promise him (Sutter) a title to the land; yet, as there were no settlements within forty miles, he was not likely to be disturbed by trespassers. Colonel Mason signed the letter, handed it to one of the gentlemen who had brought the sample of gold, and they departed. That gold was the first discovered in the Sierra Nevada, which soon revolutionized the whole country, and actually moved the whole civilized world.

... As the spring and summer of 1848 advanced, the reports came faster and faster from the gold-mines at Sutter's saw-mill. Stories reached us of fabulous discoveries, and spread throughout the land. Everybody was talking of "Gold! gold!" until it assumed the character of a fever. Some of our soldiers began to desert; citizens were fitting out trains of wagons and packmules to go to the mines. We heard of men earning fifty, five hundred, and thousands of dollars per day, and for a time it seemed as though somebody would reach solid gold. Some of this gold began to come to Yerba Buena[2] in trade, and to disturb the value of merchandise, particularly of mules, horses, tin pans, and articles used in mining: I of course could not escape the infection, and at last convinced Colonel Mason that it was our duty to go up and see with our own eyes, that we might report the truth to our Government.

… Toward the close of June, 1848, the gold-fever being at its height, by Colonel Mason's orders I made preparations for his trip to the newly-discovered gold-mines at Sutter's Fort.

… In the year 1845 a ship, the Brooklyn, sailed from New York for California, with a colony of Mormons…. As soon as the fame of the gold discovery spread through California, the Mormons naturally turned to Mormon Island, so that in July, 1848, we found about three hundred of them there at work. … I recall the scene as perfectly to-day as though it were yesterday. In the midst of a broken country, all parched and dried by the hot sun of July, sparsely wooded with live-oaks and straggling pines, lay the valley of the American River, with its bold mountain-stream coming out of the Snowy Mountains to the east. In this valley is a fiat, or gravel-bed, which in high water is an island, or is overflown, but at the time of our visit was simply a level gravel-bed of the river. On its edges men were digging, and filling buckets with the finer earth and gravel, which was carried to a machine made like a baby's cradle, open at the foot, and at the head a plate of sheet-iron or zinc, punctured full of holes. On this metallic plate was emptied the earth, and water was then poured on it from buckets, while one man shook the cradle with violent rocking by a handle. On the bottom were nailed cleats of wood. With this rude machine four men could earn from forty to one hundred dollars a day, averaging sixteen dollars, or a gold ounce, per man per day. While the sun blazed down on the heads of the miners with tropical heat, the water was bitter cold, and all hands were either standing in the water or had their clothes wet all the time; yet there were no complaints of rheumatism or cold. We made our camp on a small knoll, a little below the island, and from it could overlook the busy scene. A few bush-huts near by served as stores, boardinghouses, and for sleeping; but all hands slept on the ground, with pine-leaves and blankets for bedding.

… The next day we continued our journey up the valley of the American Fork, stopping at various camps, where mining was in progress; and about noon we reached Coloma, the place where gold had been first discovered. The hills were higher, and the timber of better quality. The river was narrower and bolder, and but few miners were at work

---

[2]San Francisco.

there, by reason of Marshall's and Sutter's claim to the site. There stood the sawmill unfinished, the dam and tail-race just as they were left when the Mormons ceased work. Marshall and Wimmer's family of wife and half a dozen children were there, guarding their supposed treasure; living in a house made of clapboards. Here also we were shown many specimens of gold, of a coarser grain than that found at Mormon Island. The next day we crossed the American River to its north side, and visited many small camps of men, in what were called the "dry diggings." Little pools of water stood in the beds of the streams, and these were used to wash the dirt; and there the gold was in every conceivable shape and size, some of the specimens weighing several ounces. Some of these "diggings" were extremely rich, but as a whole they were more precarious in results than at the river. Sometimes a lucky fellow would hit on a "pocket," and collect several thousand dollars in a few days, and then again he would be shifting about from place to place, "prospecting," and spending all he had made. Little stores were being opened at every point, where flour, bacon, etc., were sold; every thing being a dollar a pound, and a meal usually costing three dollars. Nobody paid for a bed, for he slept on the ground, without fear of cold or rain. We spent nearly a week in that region, and were quite bewildered by the fabulous tales of recent discoveries, which at the time were confined to the several forks of the American and Yuba Rivers.

3

COLONEL RICHARD MASON

Letter to Brigadier General R. Jones

August 17, 1848

Born in Virginia to an aristocratic family (one of his ancestors was George Mason, a Virginia delegate to the Constitutional Convention in 1787 who refused to sign the final document), Mason was commissioned a lieutenant in the U.S. Army at age 20 in 1817. By 1833, he was a major in the 1st U.S. Dragoons. During the Mexican-American War, he served in New Mexico and California. He was appointed military governor of California in May 1847. Whereas Mason's subordinate William Sherman confessed to being "bewildered" by the frenzied activity at the

Col. Richard B. Mason, *Report*, Monterey, California, August 17, 1848. H. ex. doc. 17, 31st Cong, 1st Sess. (January 24, 1850), 528–36.

diggings, Mason—whose report was appended to President James Polk's annual message to Congress in December 1848—pays close attention to the economics of prospecting.

Sir,—I have the honour to inform you that, accompanied by Lieut. W. T. Sherman, 3rd Artillery, A.A.A. General,[3] I started on the 12th of June last to make a tour through the northern part of California. We reached San Francisco on the 20th, and found that all, or nearly all, its male inhabitants had gone to the mines. The town, which a few months before was so busy and thriving, was then almost deserted. On the evening of the 24th the horses of the escort were crossed to Saucelito in a launch, and on the following day we resumed the journey, by way of Bodega and Sonoma, to Sutter's Fort, where we arrived on the morning of July 2. Along the whole route mills were lying idle, fields of wheat were open to cattle and horses, houses vacant, and farms going to waste. At Sutter's there was more life and business. Launches were discharging their cargoes at the river and carts were hauling goods to the fort, where already were established several stores, a hotel, etc. Captain Sutter had only two mechanics in the employe—wagon-maker and a blacksmith, whom he was then paying $10 per day. Merchants pay him a monthly rent of $100 per room, and while I was there a two-story house in the fort was rented as a hotel for $500 a month.

On the 5th we arrived in the neighbourhood of the mines, and proceeded twenty-five miles up the American Fork, to a point on it now known as the Lower Mines, or Mormon Diggings. The hill sides were thickly strewn with canvas tents and bush-harbours; a store was erected, and several boarding shanties in operation. The day was intensely hot, yet about 200 men were at work in the full glare of the sun, washing for gold—some with tin pans, some with close woven Indian baskets, but the greater part had a rude machine known as the cradle. This is on rockers, six or eight feet long, open at the foot, and its head had a coarse grate, or sieve; the bottom is rounded, with small cleets nailed across. Four men are required to work this machine; one digs the ground in the bank close by the stream; another carries it to the cradle, and empties it on the grate; a third gives a violent rocking motion to the machine, whilst a fourth dashes on water from the stream itself. The sieve keeps the coarse stones from entering the cradle, the current of water washes off the earthy matter, and the gravel is gradually carried out at the foot of the machine, leaving the gold mixed with a heavy fine black sand above

---

[3]Acting Assistant Adjutant General.

the first cleets. The sand and gold mixed together are then drawn off through auger holes into a pan below, are dried in the sun, and afterwards separated by blowing off the sand. A party of four men, thus employed at the Lower Mines, average 100 dollars a-day. The Indians, and those who have nothing but pans or willow baskets, gradually wash out the earth, and separate the gravel by hand, leaving nothing but the gold mixed with sand, which is separated in the manner before described. The gold in the Lower Mines is in fine bright scales, of which I send several specimens.

As we ascended the south branch of the American fork, the country became more broken and mountainous, and twenty-five miles below the lower washings the hills rise to about 1000 feet above the level of the Sacramento Plain. Here a species of pine occurs, which led to the discovery of the gold. Captain Sutter, feeling the great want of lumber, contracted in September last with a Mr. Marshall to build a saw-mill at that place. It was erected in the course of the past winter and spring — a dam and race constructed; but when the water was let on the wheel, the tail race was found to be too narrow to permit the water to escape with sufficient rapidity. Mr. Marshall, to save labour, let the water directly into the race with a strong current, so as to wash it wider and deeper. He effected his purpose, and a large bed of mud and gravel was carried to the foot of the race. One day Mr. Marshall, as he was walking down the race to this deposit of mud, observed some glittering particles at its upper edge; he gathered a few, examined them, and became satisfied of their value. He then went to the fort, told Captain Sutter of his discovery, and they agreed to keep it secret until a certain grist-mill of Sutter's was finished. It, however, got out and spread like magic. Remarkable success attended the labours of the first explorers, and, in a few weeks, hundreds of men were drawn thither. At the time of my visit, but little more than three months after its first discovery, it was estimated that upwards of four thousand people were employed. At the mill there is a fine deposit or bank of gravel, which the people respect as the property of Captain Sutter, though he pretends to no right to it, and would be per-fectly satisfied with the simple promise of a pre-emption on account of the mill which he has built there at a considerable cost. Mr. Marshall was living near the mill, and informed me that many persons were employed above and below him; that they used the same machines as at the lower washings, and that their success was about the same — ranging from one to three ounces of gold per man daily. ... I inquired of many if they had encountered the metal in its matrix, but in every instance they said they had not; but that the gold was invariably mixed with wash-gravel, or lodged in the crevices of other rocks. All bore testimony that they had found gold in greater or less quantities in the numerous small gullies or ravines that occur in that mountainous region.

On the 7th of July I left the mill and crossed to a small stream emptying into the American fork, three or four miles below the saw-mill. I struck the stream (now known as Weber's Creek) at the washings of Sunol and Company. They had about thirty Indians employed, whom they pay in merchandise. They were getting gold of a character similar to that found in the main fork, and doubtless in sufficient quantities to satisfy them. I send you a small specimen, presented by this Company, of their gold. From this point we proceeded up the stream about eight miles, where we found a great many people and Indians, some engaged in the bed of the stream, and others in the small side valleys that put into it. These latter are exceedingly rich, two ounces being considered an ordinary yield for a day's work. A small gutter, not more than 100 yards long by four feet wide, and two or three deep, was pointed out to me as the one where two men (W. Daly and Percy M'Coon) had a short time before obtained 17,000 dollars' worth of gold. Captain Weber informed me, that he knew that these two men had employed four white men and about 100 Indians, and that, at the end of one week's work, they paid off their party, and had left 10,000 dollars' worth of this gold. Another small ravine was shown me, from which had been taken upwards of 12,000 dollars' worth of gold. Hundreds of similar ravines, to all appearances, are as yet untouched. I could not have credited these reports had I not seen, in the abundance of the precious metal, evidence of their truth. Mr. Neligh, an agent of Commodore Stockton, had been at work about three weeks in the neighbourhood, and showed me, in bags and bottles, 2000 dollars' worth of gold; and Mr. Lyman, a gentleman of education, and worthy of every credit, said he had been engaged with four others, with a machine, on the American fork, just below Sutter's Mill, that they worked eight days, and that his share was at the rate of fifty dollars a-day, but hearing that others were doing better at Weber's Place, they had removed there, and were then on the point of resuming operations.

The country on either side of Weber's Creek is much broken up by hills, and is intersected in every direction by small streams or ravines which contain more or less gold. Those that have been worked are barely scratched, and, although thousands of ounces have been carried away, I do not consider that a serious impression has been made upon the whole. Every day was developing new and richer deposits; and the only impression seemed to be, that the metal would be found in such abundance as seriously to depreciate in value.

On the 8th July I returned to the lower mines, and eventually to Monterey, where I arrived on the 17th of July. Before leaving Sutter's,

I satisfied myself that gold existed in the bed of the Feather River, in the Yuba and Bear, and in many of the small streams that lie between the latter and the American fork; also, that it had been found in the Consumnes, to the south of the American fork. In each of these streams the gold is found in small scales, whereas in the intervening mountains it occurs in coarser lumps. Mr. Sinclair, whose rancho is three miles above Sutter's on the north side of the American, employs about fifty Indians on the north fork, not far from its junction with the main stream. He had been engaged about five weeks when I saw him, and up to that time his Indians had used simply closely-woven willow baskets. His net proceeds (which I saw) were about 16,000 dollars' worth of gold. He showed me the proceeds of his last week's work—14 lbs. avoirdupois[4] of clean-washed gold.

The principal store at Sutter's fort, that of Brannan and Co., had received in payment for goods 36,000 dollars' worth of this gold from the 1st of May to the 10th of July. Other merchants had also made extensive sales. Large quantities of goods were daily sent forward to the mines, as the Indians, heretofore so poor and degraded, have suddenly become consumers of the luxuries of life. I before mentioned that the greater part of the farmers and rancheros had abandoned their fields to go to the mines. This is not the case with Captain Sutter, who was carefully gathering his wheat, estimated at 40,000 bushels. Flour is already worth, at Sutter's, 36 dollars a-barrel, and will soon be 50. Unless large quantities of breadstuffs reach the country much suffering will occur; but as each man is now able to pay a large price, it is believed the merchants will bring from Chili and the Oregon a plentiful supply for the coming winter.

The most moderate estimate I could obtain from men acquainted with the subject was, that upwards of 4,000 men were working in the gold district, of whom more than one-half were Indians, and that from 30,000 to 50,000 dollars' worth of gold, if not more, were daily obtained. The entire gold district, with very few exceptions of grants made some years ago by the Mexican authorities, is on land belonging to the United States. It was a matter of serious reflection to me, how I could secure to the Government certain rents or fees for the privilege of securing this gold; but upon considering the large extent of country, the character of the people engaged, and the small scattered force at my command, I resolved not to interfere, but permit all to work freely, unless broils and crimes should call for interference.

The discovery of these vast deposits of gold has entirely changed the character of Upper California. Its people, before engaged in cultivating their small patches of ground, and guarding their herds of cattle and

[4]Avoirdupois is the British system of weights in which one pound equals sixteen ounces.

horses, have all gone to the mines, or are on their way thither. Labourers of every trade have left their work-benches, and tradesmen their shops; sailors desert their ships as fast as they arrive on the coast; and several vessels have gone to sea with hardly enough hands to spread a sail. Two or three are now at anchor in San Francisco, with no crew on board. Many desertions, too, have taken place from the garrisons within the influence of these mines; twenty-six soldiers have deserted from the post of Sonoma, twenty-four from that of San Francisco, and twenty-four from Monterey. I have no hesitation now in saying, that there is more gold in the country drained by the Sacramento and San Joaquin Rivers than will pay the cost of the present war with Mexico a hundred times over. No capital is required to obtain this gold, as the labouring man wants nothing but his pick and shovel and tin pan, with which to dig and wash the gravel, and many frequently pick gold out of the crevices of rocks with their knives, in pieces of from one to six ounces.

Gold is also believed to exist on the eastern slope of the Sierra Nevada; and, when at the mines, I was informed by an intelligent Mormon that it had been found near the Great Salt Lake by some of his fraternity. Nearly all the Mormons are leaving California to go to the Salt Lake; and this they surely would not do unless they were sure of finding gold there, in the same abundance as they now do on the Sacramento.

I have the honour to be,

Your most obedient Servant,

R. B. MASON, Colonel 1st Dragoons, commanding.

4

LOUISE AMELIA KNAPP SMITH CLAPP

The Shirley Letters from the California Mines
1851–1852

Louise Amelia Knapp Smith Clapp was born in New Jersey in 1819; attended academies in Charlestown and Amherst, Massachusetts; and became a schoolteacher. She and her husband, Dr. Fayette Clapp, whom she married in 1848 or 1849, sailed for California in 1849 and eventually settled in Marysville. In 1851 and 1852, Clapp wrote a series of

---

Louise Amelia Knapp Smith Clapp, *The Shirley Letters from the California Mines, 1851–52* (San Francisco: T. C. Russell, 1922), 81–82, 210–19.

letters detailing mining camp life to her sister, Molly. Around the same time, her marriage was faltering (Fayette returned east sometime in 1851 or 1852, and she filed for divorce in 1856). Her letters were later published, under the pen name "Dame Shirley," in The Pioneer, a journal edited by Ferdinand Ewer, in 1854 and 1855.

Letter the Sixth (September 30, 1851)

[I]n truth, the whole mining system in California is one great gambling or, better perhaps, lottery transaction. It is impossible to tell whether a claim will prove valuable or not. F. has invariably sunk money in every one that he has bought. Of course a man who works a claim himself is more likely, even should it turn out poor, to get his money back, as they say, than one who, like F., hires it done.

A few weeks since, F. paid a thousand dollars for a claim which has proved utterly worthless. He might better have thrown his money into the river than to have bought it, and yet some of the most experienced miners on the Bar thought that it would pay.

Letter the Fifteenth (April 10, 1852)

... [A]s to the discovery of gold. In California, at least, it must be confessed that, in this particular, science appears to be completely at fault, or as an intelligent and well-educated miner remarked to us the other day, "I maintain that science is the blindest guide that one could have on a gold-finding expedition. Those men who judge by the appearance of the soil, and depend upon geological calculations, are invariably disappointed, while the ignorant adventurer, who digs just for the sake of digging, is almost sure to be successful." I suppose that the above observation is quite correct, as all whom we have questioned upon the subject repeat, in substance, the same thing. Wherever geology has said that gold *must* be, there, perversely enough, it lies not; and wherever her ladyship has declared that it could *not* be, there has it oftenest garnered up in miraculous profusion the yellow splendor of its virgin beauty. It is certainly very painful to a well-regulated mind to see the irreverent contempt shown by this beautiful mineral to the dictates of science. But what better can one expect from the root of all evil? As well as can be ascertained, the most lucky of the mining Columbuses have been ignorant sailors, and foreigners, I fancy, are more successful than Americans.

Our countrymen are the most discontented of mortals. They are always longing for big strikes. If a claim is paying them a steady income, by which, if they pleased, they could lay up more in a month than they could in a year at home, still they are dissatisfied, and in most cases will wander off in search of better diggings. There are hundreds now pursuing this foolish course, who, if they had stopped where they first camped, would now have been rich men. Sometimes a company of these wanderers will find itself upon a bar where a few pieces of the precious metal lie scattered upon the surface of the ground. Of course they immediately prospect it, which is accomplished by panning out a few basinfuls of the soil. If it pays, they claim the spot and build their shanties. The news spreads that wonderful diggings have been discovered at such a place. The monte-dealers—those worse than fiends—rush, vulture-like, upon the scene and erect a round tent, where, in gambling, drinking, swearing, and fighting, the *many* reproduce pandemonium in more than its original horror, while a *few* honestly and industriously commence digging for gold, and lo! as if a fairy's wand had been waved above the bar, a full-grown mining town hath sprung into existence.-

But, first, let me explain to you the claiming system. As there are no state laws upon the subject, each mining community is permitted to make its own. Here they have decided that no man may claim an area of more than forty feet square. This he stakes off, and puts a notice upon it, to the effect that he holds it for mining purposes. If he does not choose to work it immediately, he is obliged to renew the notice every ten days, for, without this precaution, any other person has a right to "jump" it, that is, to take it from him. There are many ways of evading the above law. For instance, an individual can hold as many claims as he pleases if he keeps a man at work in each, for this workman represents the original owner. I am told, however, that the laborer himself can jump the claim of the very man who employs him, if he pleases so to do. This is seldom, if ever, done. The person who is willing to be hired generally prefers to receive the six dollars per diem, of which he is *sure* in any case, to running the risk of a claim not proving valuable. After all, the holding of claims by proxy is considered rather as a carrying out of the spirit of the law than as an evasion of it. But there are many ways of *really* outwitting this rule, though I cannot stop now to relate them, which give rise to innumerable arbitrations, and nearly every Sunday there is a miners' meeting connected with this subject.

Having got our gold-mines discovered and claimed, I will try to give you a faint idea of how they work them. Here, in the mountains, the labor of excavation is extremely difficult, on account of the immense rocks which form a large portion of the soil. Of course no man can work out a claim alone. For that reason, and also for the same that makes partnerships desirable, they congregate in companies of four or six, generally designating themselves by the name of the place from whence the majority of the members have emigrated; as, for example, the Illinois, Bunker Hill, Bay State, etc., companies. In many places the surface soil, or in mining phrase, the top dirt, pays when worked in a long-tom. This machine (I have never been able to discover the derivation of its name) is a trough, generally about twenty feet in length and eight inches in depth, formed of wood, with the exception of six feet at one end, called the "riddle" (query, why "riddle"?), which is made of sheet-iron perforated with holes about the size of a large marble. Underneath this colander-like portion of the long-tom is placed another trough, about ten feet long, the sides six inches, perhaps, in height, which, divided through the middle by a slender slat, is called the riffle-box. It takes several persons to manage properly a long-tom. Three or four men station themselves with spades at the head of the machine, while at the foot of it stands an individual armed "wid de shovel an' de hoe." The spadesmen throw in large quantities of the precious dirt, which is washed down to the riddle by a stream of water leading into the long-tom through wooden gutters or sluices. When the soil reaches the riddle, it is kept constantly in motion by the man with the hoe. Of course, by this means, all the dirt and gold escapes through the perforations into the riffle-box below, one compartment of which is placed just beyond the riddle. Most of the dirt washes over the sides of the riffle-box, but the gold, being so astonishingly heavy, remains safely at the bottom of it. When the machine gets too full of stones to be worked easily, the man whose business it is to attend to them throws them out with his shovel, looking carefully among them as he does so for any pieces of gold which may have been too large to pass through the holes of the riddle. I am sorry to say that he generally loses his labor. At night they pan out the gold which has been collected in the riffle-box during the day. Many of the miners decline washing the top dirt at all, but try to reach as quickly as possible the bed-rock, where are found the richest deposits of gold. The river is supposed to have formerly flowed over this bed-rock, in the crevices of which it left, as it passed away, the largest portions of the so eagerly sought for ore. The group of mountains amidst which we are living is a spur of the Sierra Nevada, and the bed-rock, which in this vicinity is of slate, is said to run through the entire range, lying, in distance varying from a few feet to eighty or ninety, beneath the surface of the soil. On Indian Bar the bed-rock falls in almost perpendicular benches, while at Rich Bar the friction of the river has formed it into large, deep basins, in which the gold, instead of being found, as you would naturally suppose, in the bottom of it, lies, for the most part, just below the rim. A good-natured individual bored *me*, and tired *himself*, in a hopeless attempt to make me comprehend that this was only a necessary consequence of the undercurrent of the water, but with my usual stupidity upon such matters I got but a vague idea from his scientific explanation, and certainly shall not mystify *you* with my confused notions thereupon.

When a company wish to reach the bed-rock as quickly as possible, they sink a shaft (which is nothing more nor less than digging a well) until they "strike it." They then commence drifting coyote-holes, as they call them, in search of crevices, which, as I told you before, often pay immensely. These coyote-holes sometimes extend hundreds of feet into the side of the hill. Of course they are obliged to use lights in working them. They generally proceed until the air is so impure as to extinguish the lights, when they return to the entrance of the excavation and commence another, perhaps close to it. When they think that a coyote-hole has been faithfully worked, they clean it up, which is done by scraping the surface of the bed-rock with a knife, lest by chance they have overlooked a crevice, and they are often richly rewarded for this precaution.

Now I must tell you how those having claims on the hills procure the water for washing them. The expense of raising it in any way from the river is too enormous to be thought of for a moment. In most cases it is brought from ravines in the mountains. A company, to which a friend of ours belongs, has dug a ditch about a foot in width and depth, and more than three miles in length, which is fed in this way. I wish that you could see this ditch. I never beheld a *natural* streamlet more exquisitely beautiful. It undulates over the mossy roots and the gray old rocks like a capricious snake, singing all the time a low song with the "liquidest murmur," and one might almost fancy it the airy and coquettish Undine herself. When it reaches the top of the hill, the sparkling thing is divided into five or six branches, each one of which supplies one, two, or three long-toms. There is an extra one, called the waste-ditch, leading to the river, into which the water is shut off at night and on Sundays. This race (another and peculiar name for it) has already cost the company more than five thousand dollars. They sell the water to others at the following rates. Those that have the first use of it pay ten per cent upon all the gold that they take out. As the water runs off from their machine (it now goes by the elegant name of "tailings"), it is taken by a company lower down, and as it is not worth so much as when it was clear, the latter pay but seven per cent. If any others wish the tailings, now still less valuable than at first, they pay four per cent on all the gold which they take out, be it much or little. The water companies are constantly in trouble, and the arbitrations on that subject are very frequent.

... Gold-mining is nature's great lottery scheme. A man may work in a claim for many months, and be poorer at the end of the time than when he commenced, or he may take out thousands in a few hours. It is a mere matter of chance. A friend of ours, a young Spanish surgeon from Guatemala, a person of intelligence and education, told us that after working a claim for six months he had taken out but six ounces.

5

JOSEPH POWNALL

Letters

1850–1854

Dr. Joseph Pownall was born in New Jersey in 1818. He journeyed overland from Louisiana to California via El Paso in 1849. After trying and failing at mining, in 1852 he joined a group of investors in the Tuolomne County Water Company. Pownall, perhaps because he spent most of his time as a failed miner digging diversion ditches, shrewdly realized that by controlling water—which miners needed to wash gold—he could see a predictable return on his investment. As rudimentary panning for gold gave way to hydraulic mining by the mid-1850s, companies that controlled reservoirs and water rights became increasingly lucrative.

Joseph Pownall to Dr. O. C. Pownall, May 1850

All the diggings operations are confined to the mountainous regions on the slope of the Sierra Nevada, now you know that the slope is not a uniform one; innumerable hills of considerable size occupy the whole face of the slope so that you are continuously ascending and discending between these hills are to be found streams of various size winding their way toward the plain below between mountains and coast. … In these mountain streams and rivers the gold is usually found.

You have come to the conclusion it may be that we can pick up a chunk of gold whenever we choose on the surface anywhere. This is a gross mistake. Imagine to yourself a stream between two mountains full of rocks and trees and stones and grass. … What is there to be done? Why you have to strike for the rocky bottom or ledge on which the stream runs and on which the gold is deposited … which often requires

Joseph Pownall Letters, 1850–1854, Joseph Pownall Collection, Huntington Library, San Marino, California.

a tremendous deal of extremely laborious work. Picture to yourself your humble servant pulling at one end of a pump endeavoring to keep a hole free while some 3 or 4 companions are at work in it.

Pownall, Hawkins Bar, August 5, 1850

I am now upon the banks of the Tuolumne River at Hawkins Bar engaged in ditching preparatory to turning the River as soon as it gets low enough which will be the case I think about the 1st Sept 1850. Thre are some 25 daming companies on the river at the present. …

This country is destined at some future day to stand out in bold relief, among the nations of the earth—its positions, climate and fine harbors give it a preeminent advantage over every competition. It has every variety of agriculture and mineral resource and I look upon it to be at no distant future day … the great link connecting United North America with vastly and densely populated Asiatic Europe and the Eastern Indies.

Pownall, Montezuma, to "my dear Thomas," January 12, 1854

The system of irrigation to which no attention has hitherto been given will undoubtedly command very soon a great deal of attention and tens of thousands of acres which are now barren wastes, the tramping ground of the wild horse, the Elk & Antelope, will become subservient to the implements of the husbandsman and be taught to produce. … The rivers leading from the mountains are short and swift, their waters can be turned easily in any direction. …

6

JOSEPH B. CHAFFEE

Letters to His Parents in Binghampton, New York
1850–1851

Chaffee was born in New York in 1830 and arrived in California via Panama in 1850. Like many failed miners, he drifted into other work: in his case, as a field hand and a logger. He was elected constable of Salmon

Joseph B. Chaffee, *Letters to His Parents in Binghampton, New York,* 1850–1851. California State Library, Sacramento.

Falls in October 1850 and was concurrently appointed a deputy county
sheriff in January 1851. He returned to New York in 1853.

July 7, 1850

We staid in Sacramento just one week and then we started for
these diggings. Salmon Falls is situated upon the South Branch of the
American River about 35 miles from Sac. City. There is quite a little
village here and a good many mines. ... The Rivers in this country do
not fall as in the States. The snow in the Mountains keeps the Rivers
high until the first or fifteenth of August.

Aug. 21, 1850, Salmon Falls

We formed ourselves into a Stock Company of 19 and since that time,
we have taken in another man so that our Co. consists of 20 shares all
Drawing Equal when they work, and when they can't they loose whatever the averages of the wages are during the time that they are sick.
Our Dividend for the last month was $275.00 after paying all debts,
dues, & demands. And we have our Canal nearly completed for turning
the River. We think that we shall do well when we get into the Bed of
the River and we have the advantage of most damming companys for we
have washed all the dirt that we took out of the canal and as you see by
the above statement got well paid for it.

October 3, 1850, Sacramento

Our dam proved a failure and after we had Prospected it thoroughly
we tore out the Race Wall and went to mining in the Bank and the next
day the River Raised 4 feet and took out almost every dam on the whole
River, North South & Middle Forks and Thousands have lost their
whole Summer's work and expenses with it. For our dam was the only
one on the whole River that I know of that got a Single cent out of their
Race where as 20 of us took about $16000.00 from the Race and Bank
together and after paying the expenses we had on average $500.

December 7, 1850, Salmon Falls

[W]hen the weather began to get stormy and cold I did not fancy mining very much so I just Hired out to Mssrs. Craig & Berry for $125.00
per month and since that time, I have been employed at most kinds of

work, the most novel of which is in this State of California ploughing. I have been breaking up Green Sward for a week past and I like it very much. My business mostly driving team. I have been drawing timber also for one week. ...

June 24, 1851, Salmon Falls

I have had nothing but my naked hands to work with since I have been here. If I had had some capital I could have done a great deal better for it is the monied men that makes the money. I am now getting a little money ahead and this fall I was going on to a 'Rancho' (farm) and lay out what money I had in Cattle & Horses and plough and put in as many acres of Barley as I can.

2

Cities

The Gold Rush spurred rapid urbanization in California: San Francisco, Sacramento, Stockton, and Marysville emerged as commercial centers for the mines. Yet not all city-building endeavors succeeded; Elisha Crosby told of his ill-fated efforts in 1849 to found the town of "Vernon" in the Sierra foothills. Towns that endured faced crises similar to those that destroyed Vernon; the physician John Morse described the cholera epidemic that beset Sacramento in 1850; he attributed the virulence of the outbreak to Californians' single-minded search for gold and consequent unwillingness to invest in hospitals or public health systems. In Sacramento (in 1850) and in San Francisco (in 1856), deadly violence erupted between factions who sought control over municipal government and lands. Charles Robinson led the Sacramento Settlers' Association in 1850; Lell Woolley was an unrepentant member of the San Francisco Vigilance Committee of 1856.

7

ELISHA OSCAR CROSBY

Memoirs

Crosby, a New York lawyer, embarked for California via Panama in December 1848. He attended the 1849 state constitutional convention, served in the state senate, worked as a lawyer in California in the 1850s, and was appointed the United States minister to Guatemala in 1861. His failed effort to establish a city at the juncture of the Feather and

Elisha Oscar Crosby Memoirs, Huntington Library.

Sacramento Rivers reminds us that just as not all prospectors found gold, not all city development schemes succeeded. The site of Vernon was later reoccupied by Indians.

The present site of Sacramento City, was then simply like the rest of the river bank, only it was a point where the embarcation and disembarcation of things was carried on from Sutter's Fort which lay about two miles back, on higher ground. ... [Sam Norris] and Frank Bates proposed to me that we purchase some land of Sutter, and lay out a town at the mouth of Feather River. We did so, buying some 1800 acres across the east bank of the Sacramento and Feather Rivers. I went up there and Superintended the laying out of the little town. ... Our town was called 'Vernon.' That was thought to be the head of navigation on the Sacramento. It assumed quite a little importance as a trading point for the Feather River miner. ... That summer it grew considerably, and in the fall of "49," it had a population of some six or seven hundred people. When the winter rains came on, that whole country was flooded, and one vast sea of water Surrounded the little Elevation where the town was situated, stretching in every direction, and boats could navigate almost anywhere across the plains. That put a quietus to the town of Vernon. Foster commenced laying out the town of Marysville that winter, on the highlands on the north side of Yuba River, and that Superseded 'Vernon' and in three or four years there was nothing left. The buildings were taken down and carried to Marysville or Sacramento.

8

DAILY ALTA CALIFORNIA

Terrible Riot at Sacramento!

August 15, 1850

The Daily Alta California *began in 1847 as the* California Star, *published by Samuel Brannan, the Mormon business magnate and founding member of the first San Francisco Vigilance Committee. Brannan was*

"Terrible Riot at Sacramento," *Daily Alta California* (August 15, 1850).

also an investor in Sacramento real estate, and thus an inveterate enemy of the squatters. Brannan sold his paper in 1848; after merging with other publications, the first issue of the Daily Alta California *appeared in January 1849. Editorially, the paper remained reliably friendly to commerce and industry.*

The long-expected collision between the land-holders and squatters has at last taken place.... An armed body of Squatters proceeded through J street about half past 1 o'clock, yesterday, and were interrupted by the authorities and opposed by portions of citizens. An affray soon commenced, and the city was aroused to arms.... Our correspondent informs us that Dr. Robinson, the leader of the squatters, was shot through the head. ... Seventeen of the squatters were killed and wounded. ... The discharge of firearms was heard in every part of the city. Martial law has been proclaimed.

9

CHARLES ROBINSON

The Sacramento Riot

1892

Charles Robinson was a Massachusetts physician who traveled overland to California in 1849. He was a committed advocate of free soil, equally opposed to slavery and in favor of the rights of white settlers to claim a portion of public land as their own. After arriving in Sacramento, he quickly found himself embroiled in squatters' opposition to the men who had founded the city and controlled both its real estate and the municipal government. He was badly wounded in the squatters riot in August 1850. Nonetheless, he enjoyed considerable popular support and was elected to a seat in the California legislature even before the charges against him for his participation in the violence were dropped. He embarked for Kansas in 1854 and became involved there in the conflict between pro- and

Charles Robinson, "The Sacramento Riot," in *The Kansas Conflict* (New York: Harper & Brothers, 1892), 37–64.

anti slavery forces over control of the territorial government. After the admission of Kansas to the Union as a free state, he served as the state's first governor from 1861 to 1863. He recounted his participation in the Sacramento riot in his 1892 autobiography, The Kansas Conflict.

Here, at the junction of the Sacramento and American rivers, seemed to be the head of navigation for shipping of all kinds, and a prosperous town was destined to grow up. ... As mining at this time was confined to the bars in the creeks and rivers, as soon as the rainy season set in these bars were covered with water, and the miners sought the towns for winter quarters. During this season, in 1849, in the absence of vegetables and variety of food, many emigrants were on the sick list, and had to be cared for by the more fortunate or suffer and die alone in their tents and cabins. These tents, shanties, and cabins, were scattered over the unoccupied lands in and around Sacramento. ... In the midst of this rainy season three men, including the Doctor, were passing along the levee between the Slough near I street and the river, when they met a pretended sheriff and posse well charged with whiskey. Curiosity caused the three men to stop and watch proceedings. The posse went directly to a structure of logs and canvas, where was a sick man who had been fed and nursed by the Doctor for several days. This man was ruthlessly hauled from his shelter, and the logs and canvas leveled with the ground. One of the three watchers exclaimed, "That is a damned outrage," and the others joined in the exclamation. It was then and there the movement commenced that culminated in the squatter riot of the next year. ... [I]t was decided to advertise a meeting to be held on the levee. ... The time for the meeting came, and with it apparently the entire population of the city. ... The speculators and their friends monopolized the speech-making till the Doctor, who was unaccustomed to public speaking, found that modesty must be ignored or the squatters' cause would be lost. After several speculators had spoken he made his way to the stand, and prefaced his resolution with an account of the situation and a statement of what he had witnessed. He then read the following preamble and resolution:

"Whereas, the land in California is presumed to be public land, therefore,

"*Resolved*, That we will protect any settler in the possession of land to the extent of one lot in the city, and one hundred and sixty acres in the country, till a valid title be shown for it."

This resolution was received with great enthusiasm.... Before adjourning, steps were taken for a permanent organization, of which the Doctor was chosen president. ...

Under Mexican rule, governors of provinces, mayors of cities, and justices of the peace were authorized to issue grants of land subject to approval by the general government. In this way, numerous grants had been made by the Governor of California, and one of eleven leagues[5] to Captain Sutter. These grants were often loosely defined, and the boundaries could be made to cover many times the amount called for in the grant. ... [I]t was such laws as these that were resorted to by the speculators to eject settlers from all northern California, claimed to be covered by Sutter's grant. At first no pretense of legal process was deemed necessary. The poor settler, who had erected his shanty or tent on some unoccupied land, would be visited by some person who would demand possession, purchase-money, or blackmail. ... The squatters' organization, when completed, played havoc with such ejectments. Either the president or some member of that association would happen at the place of ejectment and seriously interfere with the programme. The speculators, finding this game blocked, concluded to send for the Sutter title, in accordance with the demand of the squatters' platform. A certified copy was procured from the archives of Mexico and read to a large meeting called for the purpose of hearing it. But, unfortunately for the speculators, the boundaries of this pretended grant were fatally defective. The third and fourth sections of the grant read as follows:

"3d. The land of which donation is made to him is of the extent of eleven *sitios da gauado major*, as exhibited in the sketch annexed to the proceedings, without including the lands overflowed by the swelling and current of the rivers. It is bounded on the north by *los Tres Picas* (three summits) and the 39° 41' 45" of north latitude; on the east by the borders of the *Rios de las Plumas* (Feather River); on the south by the parallel 38° 49' 32" of north latitude; and on the west by the river Sacramento.

"4th. When this property shall be confirmed unto him, he shall petition the proper judge to give him possession of the land, in order that it may be measure, agreeably to ordinance, the surplus thereof remaining for the benefit of the nation, for convenient purposes."

[5] One league was 4,428 acres. The measurement was common in Texas, New Mexico, and California under Spanish and Mexican rule.

Here are natural boundaries that would seem conclusive. ... [I]t expressly excludes land overflowed by those rivers, and Sacramento was under from two to six feet of water for four or six weeks. This document, of course, confirmed the squatters in their determination to stand by each other. But the fight was not abandoned by the speculators. ... The first agency appealed to was the City Council, in December, 1849. An ordinance was passed directing certain improvements to be removed from city lots occupied by squatters. ... The president of the squatters' association, however, met them at their first job, and informed them that their authority to meddle with private property was not recognized by his association, and if they touched that property they must kill at least one person then and have a reckoning with the whole squatters' association afterwards. ... Finding that this *form* of law wouldn't frighten squatters and blood must be shed, some more impressive form must be invented. ... In the spring the president was absent several weeks in the mines, seeking a proper site for a sawmill. ... During his absence the speculators were very busy with suits, ordinances, and organizations. ...

On his return, in July, the Doctor found great discouragement among the squatters. ... [A]t length, after a search of some four or five hours, fifteen men, all told, were mustered. These were drilled for a short time. ... [and] an army of fifteen men, armed and equipped, was ready to carry into effect the resolution adopted soon after the sick man was dragged from his shelter and left exposed to the elements, eight months before. ... The squatter army of fourteen men and one commander marched in a solid column, seven abreast, down N street, with all the circumstances of grim-visaged war. ... Soon after the march was commenced, the sheriff and mayor could be seen on horseback galloping in ever direction to rally their friends to the rescue. As laboring people were released from work for dinner, many of them from curiosity joined the procession, which, by the time I street was reached was numbered by the thousand. Some were armed with rifles and shot-guns, and more with revolvers. The squatters marched and carried themselves like veterans, never breaking ranks or being disconcerted by the immense crowd at their heels. ... The squatters had but just turned the corner of J street ad Fourth, when a shout was raised and the mayor, sheriff, and their adherents opened fire, doubtless contemplating a stampede of the army of fifteen. ... No sooner was the fire of the mayor's crowd returned then all fled in hot haste. In less time than it takes to record it, the space was cleared in front of the squatters. As the mayor was on horseback, he was a shining mark, and was badly wounded, losing one arm. The city auditor, who had been very prominent and offensive, was killed.

One squatter was also killed in the first encounter. After the crowd had fled, and while the squatters were still in line, one man, named Harper, passed up J street, and when opposite the Doctor, he suddenly stopped and fired his revolver, the ball passing through the Doctor's body two inches below the heart. The Doctor then raised his rifle and returned fire, the ball striking the breast-bone of Harper and glancing of without entering the body. The next the Doctor knew, after firing at Harper, he found himself upon the ground. How he got there, or how long he had been there, he had no knowledge. ...

[I]n about three hours from the time of the encounter the Doctor was removed to the prison ship. ... Here the prisoner was left until late the next morning, evidently with no expectation on the part of the officials of any other trouble than that of a burial ... When the prisoner had partially recovered, he ... [was] taken before a so-called magistrate and formally committed on a charge of murder and other crimes ... but, after the session of the Legislature, the prisoners were discharged for want of prosecution. The prosecuting attorney would neither proceed with the trial nor enter a *nolle*,[6] and the court turned the prisoners loose.

...From the squatters' standpoint, Dr. Robinson, though wounded, was not beaten. The squatters gained their cause. Neither was the failure to prosecute because of a lack of evidence. That was abundant, but, unfortunately for the speculators, it would convict them instead of Robinson. ...

10

JOHN FREDERICK MORSE

History of Sacramento

1853

Morse was born in Essex, Vermont, in 1815, studied and practiced medicine in New York, and sailed for California via Panama in 1849. He tried mining briefly before establishing his medical practice in Sacramento.

---

[6] To enter a *nolle* is to dismiss charges.

John Frederick Morse, *History of Sacramento,* 1853 (Sacramento: Sacramento Book Collectors Club, 1945), 43–46.

A brisk trade was commencing between Sacramento and the miners. ...

[T]he long remembered Round Tent ... covered an are of about fifty feet in diameter and was the principal gambling center at the time. Music and a decorated bar and obscene pictures were the great attractions that lined this whirlpool of fortune and coerced into the vortex of penury and disgrace many an American. ...

Up to the first of August [1849] the city had enjoyed one of those strange immunities from sickness in which it was impossible to hear a sound of complaint or to witness the enfeebled and tremulous steps of convalescence. The whole community seemed in a state of health through the spring months and a portion of the summer of this eventful year. ...

All men seemed to which for was the means of setting foot upon California soil, and few were sufficiently provided in their calculations as to provide anything beyond the mere landing at S.F. Out of the thousands who landed at the above place ... not one in a hundred arrived in the country with enough money to buy a decent outfit for the mines. ... [P]enniless and destitute ... this, the great focus of mining news, the nearest trading point for miners situated upon a navigable stream, was the only place that men could think of stopping at for recuperative purposes.

... [A]t the same time that the scurvy-ridden subjects of the ocean began to concentrate amongst us, there was another more terrible train of scorbutic[7] sufferers coming in from the overland roads, so exhausted in strength and so worn out with the calamities of the journey as to be barely able to reach this, the Valley City. From these sources Sacramento became a perfect lazar house[8] of disease, suffering, and death months before anything like an effective city government was organized. It must be recollected that in proportion as these scenes began to accumulate, ust in such proportion did men seem to grow indifferent to the appeals of suffering and to the dictates of benevolence. The more urgent and importunate the cries and beseeching miseries of the sick and destitute, the more obdurate, despotic, and terrible became the reign of cupidity. Everything seemed vocal with the assurance that men came to California to make money, not to devote themselves to a useless waste of time in procuring bread and raiment for the dependent, in watching over and taking care of the sick, or in the burying of the dead. The common god (gold!) of that day taught no such feminine virtues,

[7] Afflicted with scurvy.
[8] A hospital.

and the king of the country (cupidity) declared it worse than idle in his subjects to pay attention to the ties of consanguinity. ... Fathers paid little attention to sons, and sons abandoned fathers when they requested a little troublesome care; brothers were fraternally bound to each other as long as each was equally independent of all assistance.

...The sick of the city were in consequence thrown upon the exclusive attention of a society which had become so mammon-ridden as so be almost insensible to the voices of want. Not only were the victims of scurvy evolving a general distress, but those who supposed themselves acclimated were beginning to feel the sweeping influences of miasmatic fevers which were peculiarly severe during this first season of affliction in Sacramento.

... The early setting in of the rainy season aggravated to an indescribable degree the miseries of the sick and destitute. Fevers were now making their appearance. ... [I]t was almost impossible to avoid an exhibition of scenes that would appall the heart of any man who had been reared amid the comforts and cleanliness of eastern homes. ... [D]isease was now rioting in the community.

In six days from the time of its inception, it [cholera] was making such progress that regular burials were but slightly attended to. ... The victims of the malady did not seem to be confined so much to those of intemperate and irregular habits as had been the case in almost all the previous manifestations of the disease. People of the most industrious, regular, and careful habits seemed alike vulnerable to the dreadful enemy. In a few days, many of our most substantial citizens were numbered among the victims to the sweeping epidemic. It was reported that 150 cases occurred in a single day; but such was the confusion and the positive delirium of the community that no proper records were made, nor can any accurate date now be found in respect to this epidemic of '50. As soon, however, as the daily mortality became so great as to keep men constantly employed in carrying away the dead, the citizens began to leave town in every direction and in such numbers as to soon diminish the population to probably not more than one-fifth of its ordinary standard. In this pestilential reign of terror and dismay the most dreadful abandonments of relatives and friends took place.

This awful calamity lasted in its malignant form about twenty days, but by the unsystematic records of the times the number of deaths cannot be ascertained. Besides those who died in the city, many were overtaken by death in other places and upon the road, in the desperate efforts of our citizens to escape by running for the enemy.

By the time the disease had completely disappeared, the city was nearly depopulated, and there were not a few ... that intimated that the Levee City was dead beyond a possibility of recreation.

11

HENRY A. PARKER

Letters to His Mother

1852–1853

Parker was born in Pepperell, Massachusetts, in 1832. He arrived in California in 1852, became a merchant in San Francisco, and returned to Pepperell in 1856.

December 19, 1852

The people who live in Sacramento who have so recently been afflicted by fire are now being drowned out the water having risen so high as to overflow nearly the whole city. Sacramento is situated on the San Joaquin river in a valley a levee or bank has been built along upon the bank for the purpose of preventing an overflow but the water has now risen so high as to break away the bank thus giving it a full sweep to overflow a large portion of the city thus making the sufferings of those who had been recently burned out doubly worse and destroying a large amount of property. The miners throughout the whole country are also suffering severely owing to the inclemency of the weather and the run of water which overflows them and carries away bridges, cattle, provisions, &c.

February 10, 1853

Hundreds there are here who sleep out of doors night after night in piles of hay or beside a pile of barrels lumber of something of the kind ... [W]hen a person with small means is unable to obtain employment or is taken sick he soon finds himself out of money. Thousands

Henry A. Parker, San Francisco, *Letters to His Mother in Pepperell, Massachusetts,* California State Library.

who leave their homes to come to this country have barely enough to pay their passage out here consequently they arrive here with little or no money in their pockets & as there are now hundreds in this city out of employment it makes it hard for newcomers who have not friends to assist them. They loiter about here hoping that they shall soon get employment but as they do not succeed and having spent nearly all their money, they get discouraged, take to drinking, gambling, and their sister vices & are soon completely ruined. This I am sorry to say is a true history of many a young man who left a good home to come to this country, with his heart filled with joyous expectations & high hopes which alas are dashed low & his high and lofty feelings are soon exchanged for feelings of utter disregard for himself or friends & he ends his days in misery dying a young man.

12

LELL HAWLEY WOOLEY

California

1849–1913

Wooley was born in Martinsburg, New York, in 1825. He migrated overland to California in 1849. He tried mining and hotel keeping in Grass Valley before settling in San Francisco.

Vigilance Committee of 1856

On my return to San Francisco it did not take me long to discover that the city was wide open to all sorts of crime from murder, to petty theft. ...

On May 14th, 1856, James King, editor of the "Evening Bulletin," was shot by Jas. P. Casey on the corner of Washington and Montgomery streets. He lingered along for a few days and died. This was too much for the people and proved the entering wedge for a second vigilance committee. During the first 36 hours after the shooting there were 2,600

Lell Hawley Wooley, *California, 1849–1913, or, the Rambling Sketches and Experiences of Sixty-four Years' Residence in that State* (Oakland, CA: De Witt & Snelling, 1913), 11–22.

names enrolled on the committee's books. Of that number, I am proud to say, I was the 96th member, and the membership increased until it amounted to over 7,000.

Shooting of Gen. Richardson

I will first relate a crime that had happened the November previous (November 17, 1855), in which Charles Cora had shot and killed General William H. Richardson, United States Marshal for the Northern District of California. These men had a quarrel on the evening of November 17th, 1855, between 6 and 7 o'clock, which resulted in the death of General Richardson by being shot dead on the spot in front of Fox & O'Connor's store on Clay street, between Montgomery and Leidesdorff streets, by Cora. Shortly after this Cora was arrested and placed in custody of the City Marshal. There was talk of lynching, but no resort was had to violence. Mr. Samuel Brannan delivered an exciting speech, and resolutions were declared to have the law enforced in this trial. General Richardson was a brave and honorable man, and beloved by all. He was about 33 years of age, a native of Washington, D. C., and married. Cora was confined in the County jail. We will now leave this case in the mind of the reader and take it up later on.

Shooting of James King, of William

On May 14th, 1856, the city was thrown into a great excitement by an attempt to assassinate James King, of William, editor of the "Evening Bulletin," by James P. Casey, editor of the "Sunday Times." Both Casey and King indulged in editorials of a nature that caused much personal enmity, and in one of the issues of the "Bulletin" King reproduced articles from the New York papers showing Casey up as having once been sentenced to Sing Sing. Casey took offense at the articles, and about 5 o'clock in the afternoon, at the corner of Montgomery and Washington streets, intercepted King who was on his way home, drew a revolver, saying, "Draw and defend yourself," and shot him through the left breast near the armpit. Mr. King exclaimed, "I am shot," and reeling, was caught up and carried to the Pacific Express office on the corner. Casey was quickly locked up in the station house.

Immediately following the shooting large crowds filled the streets in the neighborhood anxious to hang to the nearest lamp post the perpetrator of the crime. Casey was immediately removed to the County jail for safer keeping. Here crowds again congregated, demanding the turning over to them of Casey and threatening violence if denied. Mayor Van Ness and others addressed them in efforts to let the law take its course but the crowd which had been swelled into a seething mass, remonstrated, citing the shooting of Marshal Richardson, and demanding Cora, his assassin, that he, too, might be hanged.

Military aid was called to the defense of the jail and its prisoners and after a while the multitude dispersed, leaving all quiet.

Casey and Cora Turned Over to Vigilance Committee

Sunday, May 18th, a deputation of the Committee was delegated to call at the door of the jail and request the Sheriff to deliver up the prisoner, Casey. Upon arriving at the door three raps were made. Sheriff Scannell appeared. The delegation desired him to handcuff the prisoner and deliver him at the door. Without hesitation, the Sheriff repaired to the cell of Casey and informed him of the request of the Vigilantes. The Sheriff, after going through some preliminaries, brought the prisoner to the front door of the jail and delivered him into the hands of the Committee. My company was stationed directly across the street lined up on the sidewalk. Immediately in front of us was a small brass cannon, which a detachment had shortly before secured from the store of Macondray & Co. It was the field piece of the First California Guard. It was loaded, and alongside was the lighted match, and all was in readiness should any resistance be offered. Other companies were stationed so as to command the entire surroundings. We marched from the general headquarters of the Committee at 41 Sacramento street (Fort Gunnybags), one block from the water front, up that street to Montgomery, thence to Pacific and along Kearny to the jail, which was situated on the north side of Broadway, between Kearny and Dupont streets. Other companies came via Stockton and Dupont streets.

Casey was then ironed and escorted to a coach in waiting and, at his request, Mr. North took a seat beside him; Wm. T. Coleman and Miers F. Truett also riding in the same conveyance. Another conference was held with the Sheriff, requesting the prisoner, Charles Cora, who had murdered General Richardson, to be turned over to the Committee. Scannell declined and asked time to consider. The Committee gave the Sheriff one hour in which to decide. In less than half that time the Sheriff appeared at the door of the jail and turned Cora over to the Committee. The Committee reached the rooms on Sacramento street about 2 o'clock. Casey was placed under guard in a room above headquarters. Cora was also removed to the Committee's rooms in the same manner as Casey, the Committee having to go back to the jail for the second time. About three hundred men remained on guard at the Committee rooms after their removal there.

Fort Gunnybags

Our headquarters and committee rooms were at the wholesale liquor house of Truett & Jones, No. 41 Sacramento street, about a block from the water front, and embraced the block bounded by Sacramento, California, Front and Davis streets, and covered by brick buildings two stories high. The name "Fort Gunnybags" was ascribed to it on account of the gunnybags filled with sand which we piled up in a wall some six feet through and about ten feet high. This barricade was about twenty feet from the building. Guards were stationed at the passageways through it as well as at the stairs and doors to the buildings ... Committee by the members of the Monumental Fire Engine Company No. 6, stationed on the west side of Brenham Place, opposite the "Plaza." Our small field pieces and arms were kept on the ground floor, and the cells, executive chamber and other departments were on the second floor.

May 19th found Mr. King still suffering from his wound, but no great alarm was felt as to his condition.

Death of James King, of William

May 20th Mr. King's condition took a turn for the worse, and at 12 o'clock he was sinking rapidly, being weakened from the probing and dressing of the wound. He passed away. Sorrow and grief were shown by all. He left a widow and six children. He was born in Georgetown, D. C., and was only 34 years old.

Trial of Casey and Cora

Casey and Cora were held for trial May 20th, having been supplied with attorneys and given every opportunity to plead their cases. The Committee sat all night and took no recess until the next morning when the trials were ended. The verdict of "guilty of murder" was found in each case and they were ordered to be executed Friday, May 23rd, at 12 o'clock noon. While the trial was going on Mr. King passed away.

Hanging of Casey and Cora

The Committee, for fear that an attempt might be made to rescue Casey and Cora, arranged their companies, which numbered three thousand men and two field pieces, cleared the streets in the immediate vicinity and had constructed a platform from out of the two front windows. These platforms were hinged, the outer ends being held up by cords which were fastened to a projecting beam of the roof, to which a rope had been adjusted for the purpose of hanging.

Arabella Ryan or Belle Cora was united in marriage to Charles Cora just before the execution.

About one o'clock both Casey and Cora, who had their arms tied behind them, were brought to the platform and with firm steps stepped out upon them. Casey addressed a few remarks, declaring that he was no murderer, and weakened at the thought of his dear old mother. He almost fainted as the noose was placed around his neck. Cora, to the contrary, said nothing, and stood unmoved while Casey was talking, and apparently unconcerned. The signal was given at twenty minutes past one o'clock and the cord cut, letting the bodies drop six feet. They hung for fifty-five minutes and were cut down and turned over to the Coroner. We, the rank and file of the Vigilance Committee, were immediately afterwards drawn up in a line on Sacramento street, reviewed and dismissed after stacking our arms in the Committee room, taking up our pursuits again as private citizens. ...

Hetherington and Randall

On the evening of July 24, 1856, the Vigilance Committee had another case on their hands which called for immediate action.

Joseph Hetherington, a well-known desperate character with a previous record, picked a quarrel with Dr. Randal in the lobby of the Nicholas Hotel. They both drew their revolvers and shot: after the second report the doctor dropped and Hetherington, stooping, shot again, striking the prostrate form in the head, rendering the victim almost unconscious. He died the next morning.

The shooting was brought about through Randal's inability to repay money borrowed from Hetherington on a mortgage on real estate.

Hetherington, who was captured by the police, had been turned over to the Committee by whom he was tried, the Committee going into session immediately after the shooting, found him guilty of murder and sentenced him to be hanged.

We were again called out on the 29th and were stationed so as to command the situation. This time a gallows was erected on Davis street, between Sacramento and Commercial.

Another man, Philander Brace by name, was also to be hanged at the same time, and at about 5:30 in the afternoon of July 29th they were both conveyed in carriages, strongly guarded, to the execution grounds. Hetherington had previously proclaimed his innocence, claiming that the Doctor had shot first and he had simply shot in self-defense, but his previous record was bad, he having killed a Doctor Baldwin in 1853 and had run a gambling joint on Long Wharf, and eye witnesses claimed that he not only provoked but shot first.

Brace was of a different nature, he was a hardened criminal of a low type. The charge against him being the killing of Captain J. B. West about a year previous, out in the Mission, and of murdering his accomplice. He had also confessed to numerous other crimes.

Hanging of Hetherington and Brace

Thousands of people were on the house-tops and in windows and on every available spot from which a view of the gallows was to be had. The prisoners mounted the scaffold, being accompanied by three Vigilance Committee officers who acted as executioners and a Rev. Mr. Thomas. After the noose had been adjusted, Hetherington addressed the crowd, claiming to be innocent, and ready to meet his Maker. Brace, every once in a while, interrupted him, using terrible and vulgar language. The caps were adjusted, the ropes cut and the two dropped into eternity. They were left hanging 40 minutes, after which the bodies were removed by the Committee to their rooms and afterwards turned over to the Coroner. They were both young men—Hetherington 35, a native of England, had been in California since 1850, while Brace was but 21, a native of Onandaigua County, N. Y.

Ballot Box Stuffing

The ballot boxes that had been used by Casey and his ilk were of a peculiar construction, having false slides on the sides and bottoms that could be slipped out and thereby letting enough spurious votes drop into the box to insure the election of their man or men. It was claimed that nearly the entire set of municipal officers then holding office had secured their election through this man. They were afterwards requested by the Vigilance Committee to resign their offices, but at the first election that was held on November 4th, they were all displaced by men selected by a new party (the People's party) that was the outcome of the efforts of the Vigilance Committee. ...

Black List

From the book entitled "San Francisco Vigilance Committee of '56," by F. W. Smith, I quote the following, with some corrections and alterations:

"I am informed by an ex-Vigilante that the Committee roll call of '56, just before its disbandment, numbered between eight and nine thousand.

In concluding our history of this society, we will give the names and penalties inflicted on those who came under its eye during the latter year; whose conduct was so irreparably bad that it could not be excused. Those who suffered the death penalty did so in expiation for lives they had taken. The names of these culprits are familiar to the reader. We also give the names of those who were required to leave the State; all of whom, in the archives of the Vigilantes, fall under the head of the black list:"

James P. Casey, executed May 22nd, 1856.

Charles Cora, executed May 22nd, 1856.

Joseph Hetherington, executed July 29th, 1856.

Philander Brace, executed July 29th, 1856.

Yankee Sullivan (Francis Murray), suicided May 31st, 1856.

Chas. P. Duane, shipped on "Golden Age," June 5th, 1856.

William Mulligan, shipped on "Golden Age," June 5th, 1856.

Wooley Kearney, shipped on "Golden Age," June 5th, 1856.

Bill Carr, sent to Sandwich Islands, June 5th, 1856, bark "Yankee."

Martin Gallagher, sent to Sandwich Island, June 5th, 1856, bark "Yankee."

Edward Bulger, sent to Sandwich Islands, June 5th, 1856, bark "Yankee."

Peter Wightman, ran away about June 1st, 1856.

Ned McGowan, ran away about June 1st, 1856.

John Crow, left on "Sonora," June 20th, 1856.

Bill Lewis, shipped on "Sierra Nevada," June 20th, 1856.

Terrence Kelley, shipped on "Sierra Nevada," June 20, 1856.

John Lowler, shipped on "Sierra Nevada," June 20th, 1856.

William Hamilton, shipped on "Sierra Nevada," June 20th, 1856.

James Cusick, ordered to leave but refused to go, and fled into the interior.

James Hennessey, ordered to leave, but fled to the interior.

T. B. Cunningham, shipped July 5th, 1856, on "John L. Stephens."

Alex. H. Purple, shipped July 5th, 1856, on "John L. Stephens."

Torn Mulloy, shipped July 5th, 18,56, on "John L. Stephens."

Lewis Mahoney, shipped July 5, 1856, on "John L. Stephens."

J. R. Maloney, shipped July 5th, 1856, on "John L. Stephens."

Dan'l Aldrich, shipped July 5th, 1856, on "John L. Stephens."

James White, Shipped July 21st, 1856, on "Golden Age."

James Burke, alias "Activity," shipped July 21st, 1856, on "Golden Age."

Wm. F. McLean, shipped July 21st, 1856, on "Golden Age."

Abraham Kraft, shipped July 21st, 1856, on "Golden Age."

John Stephens, shipped September 5, 1856, on "Golden Age."

James Thompson, alias "Liverpool Jack," shipped September 5, 1856, on "Golden Age."

Many others either left of their own volition or under orders to leave the state.

Bulger and Gallagher who had been shipped out of the country on June 5th returned to San Francisco. In their haste the Committee had failed to read their sentences to them and they were not aware of the penalty of returning. They were again shipped out of the country and ordered not to return under penalty of death.

There were 489 persons killed during the first 10 months of 1856. Six of these were hanged by the Sheriff, and forty-six by the mobs, and the balance were killed by various means by the lawless element.

3

The National and Transnational Context
of the Gold Rush

The California gold rush belongs to both national and international contexts. California was very much a part of national politics: its admission to the Union was part of the Compromise of 1850, in which California, a large free state, balanced the admission in 1845 of Texas, a large slave state. Yet the politics of slavery remained active in California. Although California legislators overwhelmingly approved applying for admission to the Union as a free state, they also sought to bar free blacks from the state. And California made little effort to prevent slave-owners from bringing slaves into the state, or from returning them to slavery in the South. The gold rush was also a transnational phenomenon: it attracted laborers not only from the United States but from Europe, Latin America, and the Pacific world. In 1849, one-quarter of the California population had been born outside of the United States. And while the discovery of gold in California initiated the first modern gold rush, it was followed shortly thereafter by discoveries in Australia, New Zealand, and British Columbia. American miners moved from California to new goldfields in western Canada, Australia, and New Zealand—all parts of the British Empire. Each of these gold rushes attracted prospectors from around the world. In numerous respects, the California Gold Rush belongs to a larger, multi-national, Anglophone circum-Pacific world of gold rushes.

13

CALIFORNIA CONSTITUTIONAL CONVENTION
Debates
1849

In June 1849, Gen. Bennett Riley, California's fifth military governor in ten months, called for a constitutional convention in Monterey. The convention, dominated by Americans who had migrated to California before 1847, began its work in September and completed it in six weeks; California voters promptly approved the constitution in November 1849 by a vote of 12,064 to 811. Reflecting national politics, convention delegates opposed both slavery and the presence of free blacks in the state—in both instances, the fact that African Americans performed the same work as white laborers in the mines and elsewhere was thought to be degrading to white workers. After approving the final document, California's petition for statehood languished in Washington for nearly a year, while Congress wrangled over the admission of another free state.

Mr. SHANNON moved to insert, as an additional section, the following:

> Neither slavery nor involuntary servitude, unless for the punishment of crimes, shall ever be tolerated in this State.

Mr. CARVER moved to amend the amendment, by adding thereto the following:

> Nor shall the introduction of free negroes, under indentures or otherwise, be allowed.

After debate as to the propriety of a division of the two questions, Mr. CARVER withdrew his amendment.

Mr. Shannon's amendment then being first in order, Mr. HALLECK, after debate in reference to the particular portion of the Constitution which the provision should appear in, moved that "a declaration against the introduction of slavery into California shall be inserted in the bill

J. Ross Browne, *Report of the Debates of the Convention of California, on the Formation of the State Constitution* (Washington, DC: J. T. Towers, 1850), 43–44, 48–50.

of rights," Mr. Shannon temporarily withdrawing his amendments to enable Mr. Halleck to make the motion.

The motion of Mr. Halleck was decided in the affirmative.

Mr. SHANNON then again submitted his amendment, and after further debate as to the expediency of submitting the question to the people in a separate article, the proposed section was *unanimously adopted.* ...

Mr. McCARVER had an amendment which he desired to offer as an additional section. It was in the following words:

> SEC. 19. The Legislature shall, at its first session, pass such laws as will effectually prohibit free persons of color from immigrating to and settling in this State, and to effectually prevent the owners of slaves from bringing them into this State for the purpose of setting them free.

He deemed this necessary because the House had already made a provision prohibiting the introduction of slavery, the object of which he thought would be defeated by a system already in practice. He had heard of gentlemen having sent to the States for their negroes, to bring them here, on condition that they should serve for a specified length of time. He was informed that many had been liberated with this understanding. After serving a few years, they were to be set loose on the community. He protested against this. If the people of this Territory are to be free against the curse of slavery, let them also be free from the herds of slaves who are to be set at liberty within its borders. He wished to have the sense of the House on this question. If the subject was neglected now, it would soon be necessary to alter the Constitution. In Illinois, this question was laid before the people in a separate article, and a majority of twenty thousand of the voters of that State supported it. Have we not greater reason to fear the introduction of free negroes here, than they had in Illinois? The slave owner, possessed of a hundred negroes, can well afford to liberate them, if they engage to serve him for three years. What is to support them after that? Are they to be thrown upon the community? He believed that if any State in the Union required protection from this class of people, it was California. It is the duty of gentlemen to make provision in this Constitution against the introduction of negro labor, as well as prohibit the introduction of slavery.

Mr. WOZENCRAFT said:

> Mr. President: We have declared, by a unanimous vote, that neither slavery nor involuntary servitude shall ever exist in this State. I desire now to cast my vote in favor of the proposition just

submitted, prohibiting the negro race from coming amongst us; and this I profess to do as a philanthropist, loving my kind, and rejoicing in their rapid march toward perfectability.

If there was just reason why slavery should not exist in this land, there is just reason why that part of the family of man, who are so well adapted for servitude, should be excluded from amongst us. It would appear that the all-wise Creator has created the negro to serve the white race. We see evidence of this wherever they are brought in contact; we see the instinctive feeling of the negro is obedience to the white man, and, in all instances, he obeys him, and is ruled by him. If you would wish that all mankind should be free, do not bring the two extremes in the scale of organization together; do not bring the lowest in contact with the highest, for be assured the one will rule and the other must serve.

I wish to cast my vote against the admission of blacks into this country, in order that I may thereby protect the citizens of California in one of their most inestimable rights—the right to labor. This right is not only valuable, but it is a holy commandment—"by the sweat of thy brow shalt thou earn thy daily bread." I wish to inculcate this command, and encourage labor. I wish, so far as my influence extends, to make labor honorable; the laboring man is the *nobleman* in the true acceptation of the word; and I would make him worthy of his high prerogative, and not degrade him by placing him upon a level with the lowest in the scale of the family of man. I would remove all obstacles to his future greatness, for if there is one part of the world, possessing advantages over another, where the family of Japhet may expect to attain a higher state of perfectability than has ever been attained by man, it is here, in California. All nature proclaims this a favored land. The assertion that we would be unjust in excluding that part of the human race from coming here, has no foundation in reason. We must be just to ourselves—by so doing we avoid injustice to others. In claiming the right to labor we do not deny the same to others. The African is well fitted for labor, you would say. Why deny him our field? Sir, we do not deny him the right to labor; we are willing that he should have the boundless wastes of his native land for his field—a region where the all-wise Creator, in his wisdom, saw fit to place him; but we are not willing that he should be placed in our field, where, instead of good to either party, evil would come to both. We are not only reasonable but we are just. No one will deny that a free black population is one of the greatest evils that can afflict society. We know it to be so. We have witnessed enough to know it and deplore it. There is not an advocate for the admission of blacks that would be willing to take the negro by the hand in fellowship—that would be willing to extend to him the right of suffrage—that would be willing to admit him on a footing in our political or social confederacy. Is it just, then, to encourage by our silence the emigration of a class of beings who at best are dead weights in society—resting on our social institutions like an incubus of darkness?

I desire to protect the people of California against all monopolies—to encourage labor and protect the laboring class. Can this be done by admitting the negro race? Surely not; for if they are permitted to come, they will do so—nay they will be brought here. Yes, Mr. President, the capitalists will fill the land with these living laboring machines, with all their attendant evils. Their labor will go to enrich the few, and improverish the many; it will drive the poor and honest laborer from the field, by degrading him to the level of the negro. The vicious propensities of this class of population will be a heavy tax on the people. Your officers will have to be multiplied; your prisons will have to be doubled; your society will corrupted. Yes, sirs, you will find when it is too late that you have been saddled with an evil that will gall you to the quick, and yet it cannot be thrown off. You can prevent it now by passing this section. It should be done now. Do not wait for legislative enactment—the Legislature may, and doubtless will, pass laws effectually to prevent blacks from coming, or being brought here, but it will be an extended evil even at that date. When this Constitution goes forth without a prohibitionary clause relative to blacks you will see a black-tide setting in here and spreading over the land; you will see a greater curse than the locusts of Egypt. This is no fancy sketch—it is a plain assertion, based on a just knowledge of things, which requires no gift of prophecy to foresee. If you fail to pass this bill you will have cause to revert to my assertions.

The future, to us, is more promising than that of any State that has ever applied for admission into the Union. The golden era is before us in all its glittering splendor; here civilization may attain its highest altitude; Art, Science, Literature will here find a fostering parent, and the Caucasian may attain his highest state of perfectibility. This is all before us. It is within our reach; but to attain it we must pursue the path of wisdom. We must throw aside all the weights and clogs that have fettered society elsewhere. We must inculcate moral and industrial habits. We must exclude the low, vicious, and depraved. Every member of society should be on a level with the mass—able to perform his appropriate duty. Having his equal rights, he should be capable of maintaining those rights, and aiding in their equal diffusion to others. There should be that equilibrium in society which pervades all nature, and that equilibrium can only be established by acting in conformity with the laws of nature. There should be no incongruities in the structure; it should be a harmonious whole, and there should be no discordant particles, if you would have a happy unity. That the negro race is out of his social sphere, and becomes a discordant element when among the Caucasian race, no one can doubt. You have but to take a retrospective view, and you need not extend your vision beyond our own land to be satisfied of this fact. Look at our once happy republic, now a contentious, antagonistical, discordant people. The Northern people see, and feel, and know, that the black population is an evil in the land, and although they have admitted them to many of the rights of citizenship, the admixture has acted in the political economy as a foreign, poisonous substance, producing the same effect as in physical economy—derangement, disease, and, if not removed, *death*. Let us be warned—let us avoid an evil of such magnitude.

I will trespass on the patience of the House no further, Mr. President, than to express the wish that this clause may become an article in the Constitution.

14

SAN FRANCISCO BULLETIN

Stovall v. Archy, a Slave

February 13, 1858

In 1857, Charles Stovall brought his slave, Archy Lee, from Mississippi to California, where he hired out Archy as a laborer. When Stovall attempted to return Archy to Mississippi, free blacks in Sacramento, led by Charles Parker, hid Archy and later filed a petition for writ of habeus corpus, alleging that under California law Archy was being unlawfully held. In 1858, the Sacramento County Court ruled that because of the length of Stovall's residence in California, the Fugitive Slave Law of 1850 did not apply and that Archy was free. The California Supreme Court reversed that decision, however, arguing, in effect, that Stovall had made an innocent mistake in bringing his slave to a free state. When Stovall subsequently attempted to remove Archy from California via San Francisco, free blacks once more intervened with another petition for writ of habeus corpus. The case went before a U.S. Commissioner who ruled in Archy's favor.

The Supreme Court gave a decision on the 11th of February, in the fugitive slave matter, arising in the case of the negro "Archy," on *habeus corpus*. In a lengthy, and very likely an able opinion, the Court decide[d] against every position taken by the petitioner, C. A. Stovall; but, strange to say—if anything can be strange in this country—finally concluded to turn over the prisoner Archy, to his old master, in order that he may take the negro back to Mississippi! This is extraordinary but true—"a most lame and impotent conclusion" indeed. The opinion is written by Justice Burnett, Chief-Justice Terry concurring. Their own words tell this curious judicial tale. They are as follows:

> From the views we have expressed, it would seem *clear* that the petitioner cannot sustain either the character of traveler or visitor. But there are circumstances connected with this particular case, that may exempt him from the operation of the rules we have laid down. This is the first case that has occurred under the existing law; and from the opinion of Mr. Justice Anderson, and the silence of the Chief Justice, the petitioner had some reason to believe that the constitutional provision would have no immediate operation. Besides this consideration, the petitioner is a young man, traveling mainly for his health. This being the first case, and under these circumstances, we are not disposed to rigidly enforce the rule *for the first time*. But in reference to all future cases, it is our purpose to enforce the rules laid down strictly, according to their true intent and spirit.

> It is therefore ordered that Archy be forthwith released from the custody of the Chief of Police, and given into the custody of the petitioner, Charles A. Stoval.

> –Burnett, J.

> I concur in the judgment, and in the principles announced in the opinion of my associate; while I do not entirely agree with his conclusions from the facts of the case. I think the delay of the petitioner was unavoidable, and that the fact of his engaging in labor in order to support himself during his necessary detention, did not divest his rights under the law of comity, as laid down in the opinion.

> –Terry, C. J.

15

VICENTE PÉREZ ROSALES

Times Gone By

1882

Pérez Rosales, born in Santiago, Chile, in 1807, was a member of Chile's wealthy, educated elite. He was privately tutored in Chile and then studied in Paris between 1825 and 1830. After returning to Chile, he tried his hand at farming, shopkeeping, and journalism. In December 1848 he, together with four brothers and a brother-in-law, left Chile for California.

For Chileans, California was an unknown country. ... Some friends had impressed on us the need to go armed, and always at least two of us at a time. We followed this advice and saw that most of the local traders were also armed, displaying not only their goods but also a knife at their side or a revolver. ... The inhabitants [of San Francisco], of the most varied nationalities, came to 1,500 residents and that many more transients, and seemed to be celebrating an immense and boisterous masked ball, to judge by their exotic costumes, the variety of their languages, and the very nature of their occupations. Even the women seemed to have dressed as men, because no matter how much you looked for a skirt in that madhouse, you could see nothing like it to save your life. The fringed leather jacket of the tough-looking Oregonian, the peaked Chilean cap, the parasol-like hat of the Chinese, the huge boots of the Russians that seemed to be swallowing their owners, the Frenchman, the Englishman, the Italian disguised as a sailor, the yokel in a frock coat about to breathe its last, the gentleman with no coat, in a word, everything you might find in a gigantic carnival was to be seen there, and in dizzying motion.

When we got there, the village at the Mill consisted of a store, two wooden huts, and many canvas and leaf shelters scattered hither and yon. It was, however, no longer considered the main mining site. What the miner looked for was an as yet unexplored place; and therefore many barely stopped here and went on to the Middle and North Forks, concerning

---

Vicente Pérez Rosales, *Times Gone By: Memoirs of a Man of Action*. [Recuerdos del pasado, 1882] (New York: Oxford University Press, 2003), 217, 228–29, 253–54, 258–59, 271–72.

which such wonderful tales were told. Still, there was no lack of gold at the Mill; if people had come to disdain it, it was because at that time nobody wanted to work at looking for gold instead of just walking up and finding it.

The day after pitching our camp, we all set out in a merry procession, each man carrying his pan, his scoop, his shovels, and his crowbars. After walking for a while along the river bank among the debris of recent excavations, we decided to try our hand as best we could, to get some experience in the use of the pan. For two hours we alternately scraped, hauled, and washed, and netted an ounce and a half of gold; whereupon, deeming ourselves sufficiently trained, we ate our tasty beans and then proceeded to choose a spot on which to set up our operations in earnest. We found it on one of the steep banks carved out by the river, where an extensive bed of sand and gravel lay under a foot or so of soil. As soon as we scratched the ground next to the water, we saw to our delight that many bits of gold sparkled there; and after estimating how far that gold deposit might stretch, and in what direction, we immediately took possession of it, leaving two of our number to sleep there with their weapons as guards of this treasure.

I must say that our harvest was exceedingly meager for the first three days, because we were panning by hand; but we soon acquired a California cradle, and, as we lovingly rocked our golden baby, we saw it grow prodigiously. This very simple but ingenious device, which has all the advantages of a gigantic miner's scoop, consists of an ordinary cradle about a yard and a half in length and half a yard wide, placed so that its head rests on a base about a span higher than that of the foot.

... The method for using this primitive but most useful contraption is so easy and effortless that after watching it in operation for even a short while the most ignorant bystander can claim to be an expert. One man deposits gold-bearing soil on the screen, another pours buckets of water on it, a third rocks the cradle, and the last removes by hand the stones too large to pass through the screen, examines them, and if no gold is to be seen in them, throws them away. The water turns the soil on the screen into mud, which runs down the inclined plane; and the gold, along with other more or less heavy objects, is trapped by the wooden cross strips. The operation is interrupted every ten minutes to collect the gold dust and nuggets that, mixed with iron, have gathered in the angles formed by the strips; the yield is then deposited in a pan, to be further purified at night, and the operation goes on until day's end. Once we began to use the cradle, our daily harvest varied between ten and twenty-two ounces of gold. ...

The relations between Chileans and Americans were far from cordial. ... The hostility of the common run of Yankees toward the sons of other nations, and most especially toward Chileans, had intensified.

Their argument was simple and conclusive: the Chilean descended from the Spaniard, the Spaniard had Moorish blood, therefore the Chilean had to be at the least a Hottentot or at best something very much like the timid and abased Californio.

16

EDWARD HARGRAVES

Australia and Its Gold Fields

1855

Hargraves was born in England in 1816, went to sea at age 14, and arrived in Sydney, Australia, in 1832. In Australia, he worked as a farmer and a shipping company agent; married; squandered his wife's money; and in 1849 embarked for California. He had little success in California, but upon returning to Sydney in 1851, he was determined to claim a reward of £10,000 offered by the Australian government to anyone who could discover a payable gold field. He found only a few specks, but nonetheless in early May 1851 he trumpeted the discovery in an area he named Ophir. By the middle of May there were 300 prospectors in Ophir and the Australian gold rush had begun.

[T]he news of the discovery of gold on the west coast of North America, in the autumn of 1848 ... excited the inhabitants of Australia—men who for the most part have spent their whole lives in adventure, in varied and more or less hazardous enterprise. ... [A]fter a little consideration, I took my passage for San Francisco. ...

We fell in with people from all parts of Europe and America; with our own countrymen from Australia, with Frenchmen, Spaniards, Portuguese, Mexicans, Chilians, Peruvians, and those from the various states of America. ...

We worked for gold in the drift overlaying the slates, and also found gold in the laminae of these rocks; the largest deposits commonly rested

---

Edward Hargraves, *Australia and Its Gold Fields* (London: Ingram, 1855), 72, 74, 88–90, 96, 111, 114–16.

in the indentations and cavities of the slates. ... It was now that for the first time I ventured to put in writing my belief in the existence of gold in New South Wales. My confidence in the conclusion I had come to was never for a moment shaken, but ... I was unwilling, after having taken so long a voyage in search of fortune, to return no richer than I came; added to which, during a considerable portion of my sojourn in California I was gaining experience which would stand me in good stead, whenever I should commence my searches for gold in Australia. ...

I set sail for Port Jackson [Sydney] ... bent on making that discovery which had so long occupied my thoughts, and reached that place in January, 1851. ... [O]n the 5th of February I set out from Sydney on horseback alone to cross the Blue Mountains. ... I found myself in the country that I was so anxiously longing to behold again. My recollection of it had not deceived me. The resemblance of its formation to that of California could not be doubted or mistaken. I felt myself surrounded by gold; and with tremulous anxiety panted for the moment of trial, when my magician's wand should transform his trackless wilderness into a region of countless wealth. ... I took the pick and scratched the gravel off a schistose dyke, which ran across the creek at right angles with its side; and, with a trowel, I dug a panful of earth, which I washed in the water-hole. The first trial produced a little piece of gold. "Here it is!" I exclaimed; and I then washed five panfuls in succession, obtaining gold from all but one.

No further proof was necessary.

17

JOHN T. KNOW

Letter to the Sacramento Daily Union

May 31, 1858

Know was one of thousands of Americans who left California for the Fraser River Gold Rush in British Columbia in 1857–1858.

John T. Know, Whatcom, British Columbia, to the *Sacramento Daily Union*, May 31, 1858.

Before leaving Sacramento, I promised several friends that when I arrived here, and saw how things looked, I would write and inform them of all the information I could obtain concerning the gold mines of Fraser River. Then, to begin with, I will say, that I have seen and conversed with quite a number of gentlemen who have visited the mines, and all agree that they are very rich; but owing to the high water, there has been very little done, but enough, however, to satisfy all that I have conversed with that when the water falls, so the bars can be worked, the pay will be large. The water will not fall in Fraser River, so that the bars can be worked to advantage, before the first of July. The miners have been pouring in here at a great rate, calculating to go up the road that is being cut from here to Thompson River. The road, however, is not yet completed; in consequence of which, the miners generally fit out here with small boats and canoes, and push off up Fraser River. Provisions are plenty and cheap here, so that those who come need have no fears about getting their supplies at this point, and at as cheap rates as they can buy at San Francisco and pay the exorbitant freight charged by the steamship company. There is quite a diversity of opinion as to whether this point of Victoria will be the great depot for the new gold mines. At present, this place has the advantage; but whether it will continue so or not, I am unable to say. If the road can be made as good as reports say it can, I see no good reason why this should not be the starting point. It is about one hundred and fifty miles from here by land to the mines, and about three hundred by the river route. This place is situated on Bellingham Bay, some forty miles south of the mouth of Fraser River. It is a beautiful site for a city, well watered with the best spring water, and timbered over as thick as can be, with pine and cedar. The town is building up rapidly, after the fashion of your mining towns, with shanties and canvas tents.

4

Californios

Before the Mexican-American War, Alta Calfornia was a Mexican province dominated by cattle ranches. Most of the rancheros, who had received large land grants from the Mexican government in the 1830s and early 1840s, were Mexicans, but roughly one-third were from the United States or western Europe. Richard Henry Dana, a sailor, described the cattle industry and the social life of the Californios in 1840. The letters of Abel Stearns, Cave Johnson Couts, and Charles Johnson—all Americans who married into an established Californio family in Los Angeles—between 1852 and 1857 chart the efforts of the Californios to adapt to the Gold Rush, particularly their effort to supply beef to the miners. A notable challenge to the Californios was the U.S. Land Commission, which, beginning in 1851, judged the legality of over 800 Mexican grants. The commission confirmed about 75 percent of the grants, but the litigation costs were sometimes ruinous. The eclipse of the Californios is likewise evident in the 1859 will of Juan Bandini, a prominent ranchero whom Dana had met years earlier.

18

RICHARD HENRY DANA

Two Years Before the Mast

1840

Dana was born in Cambridge, Massachusetts, in 1815, into a family that had arrived in the Massachusetts Bay Colony in 1640. His family's connections and academic ambitions determined that he was tutored by

Richard Henry Dana, *Two Years Before the Mast*, 1840 (New York: Signet, 1981), 117–32, 311–12.

Ralph Waldo Emerson before entering Harvard. He left Harvard after contracting measles, however, and in 1834 he signed on as a seaman aboard the Pilgrim *bound for California. He returned to Massachusetts in 1836, took a law degree from Harvard in 1837, and became a prominent abolitionist. His account of his two years as a seaman was published in 1840.*

After a few days we made the land at Point Pinos, which is the headland at the entrance of the bay of Monterey. ... The shores are extremely well wooded (the pine abounding upon them), and as it was now the rainy season, everything was as green as nature could make it,—the grass, the leaves, and all; the birds were singing in the woods, and great numbers of wild fowl were flying over our heads. Here we could lie safe from the southeasters. We came to anchor within two cable lengths of the shore, and the town lay directly before us, making a very pretty appearance; its houses being of whitewashed adobe, which gives a much better effect than those of Santa Barbara, which are mostly left of a mud color. The red tiles, too, on the roofs, contrasted well with the white sides, and with the extreme greenness of the lawn upon which the houses—about a hundred in number—were dotted about, here and there, irregularly. There are in this place, and in every other town which I saw in California, no streets nor fences (except that here and there a small patch might be fenced in for a garden), so that the houses are placed at random upon the green. This, as they are of one story, and of the cottage form, gives them a pretty effect when seen from a little distance.

It was a fine Saturday afternoon that we came to anchor, the sun about an hour high, and everything looking pleasantly. The Mexican flag was flying from the little square Presidio, and the drums and trumpets of the soldiers, who were out on parade, sounded over the water, and gave great life to the scene. Every one was delighted with the appearance of things. We felt as though we had got into a Christian (which in the sailor's vocabulary means civilized) country. ...

The Californians are an idle, thriftless people, and can make nothing for themselves. The country abounds in grapes, yet they buy, at a great price, bad wine made in Boston and brought round by us, and retail it among themselves at a real (12 1/2 cents) by the small wineglass. Their hides, too, which they value at two dollars in money, they barter for something which costs seventy-five cents in Boston; and buy shoes (as like as not made of their own hides, which have been carried twice round Cape Horn) at three and four dollars, and "chicken-skin boots" at fifteen dollars a pair. Things sell, on an average, at an advance of nearly three hundred per cent upon the Boston prices. This is partly owing to the heavy duties which the government, in their wisdom, with an idea, no doubt, of keeping the silver in the country, has laid upon imports. These duties, and the enormous expenses of so long a voyage, keep all merchants but those of heavy capital from engaging in the trade. Nearly two thirds of all the articles imported into the country from round Cape Horn, for the last six years, have been by the single house of Bryant, Sturgis, & Co., to whom our vessel belonged. ...

The fondness for dress among the women is excessive, and is sometimes their ruin. A present of a fine mantle, or of a necklace or pair of ear-rings, gains the favor of the greater part. Nothing is more common than to see a woman living in a house of only two rooms, with the ground for a floor, dressed in spangled satin shoes, silk gown, high comb, and gilt, if not gold, ear-rings and necklace. ...

Monterey, as far as my observation goes, is decidedly the pleasantest and most civilized-looking place in California. In the centre of it is an open square, surrounded by four lines of one-story buildings, with half a dozen cannon in the centre; some mounted, and others not. This is the Presidio, or fort. Every town has a presidio in its centre; or rather every presidio has a town built around it; for the forts were first built by the Mexican government, and then the people built near them, for protection. The presidio here was entirely open and unfortified. There were several officers with long titles, and about eighty soldiers, but they were poorly paid, fed, clothed, and disciplined. ...

In Monterey there are a number of English and Americans (English or Ingles all are called who speak the English language) who have married Californians, become united to the Roman Church, and acquired considerable property. Having more industry, frugality, and enterprise than the natives, they soon get nearly all the trade into their hands. They usually keep shops, in which they retail the goods purchased in larger quantities from our vessels, and also send a good deal into the interior, taking hides in pay, which they again barter with our ships. In every town on the coast there are foreigners engaged in this kind of trade, while I recollect but two shops kept by natives. The people are naturally suspicious of foreigners, and they would not be allowed to remain, were it not that they conform to the Church, and by marrying natives, and bringing up their children as Roman Catholics and Mexicans, and not teaching them the English language, they quiet suspicion, and even become popular and leading men. The chief alcaldes in Monterey and Santa Barbara were Yankees by birth.

The men in Monterey appeared to me to be always on horseback. Horses are as abundant here as dogs and chickens were in Juan

Fernandez. There are no stables to keep them in, but they are allowed to run wild and graze wherever they please, being branded, and having long leather ropes, called lassos, attached to their necks and dragging along behind them, by which they can be easily taken. The men usually catch one in the morning, throw a saddle and bridle upon him, and use him for the day, and let him go at night, catching another the next day. When they go on long journeys, they ride one horse down, and catch another, throw the saddle and bridle upon him, and, after riding him down, take a third, and so on to the end of the journey. There are probably no better riders in the world. ... They frequently give exhibitions of their horsemanship. ...

Wednesday, January 6th, 1836. Set sail from Monterey, with a number of Mexicans as passengers, and shaped our course for Santa Barbara. The Diana went out of the bay in company with us, but parted from us off Point Pinos, being bound to the Sandwich Islands. We had a smacking breeze for several hours, and went along at a great rate until night, when it died away, as usual, and the land-breeze set in, which brought us upon a taut bowline. Among our passengers was a young man who was a good representation of a decayed gentleman. He reminded me much of some of the characters in Gil Blas.[9] He was of the aristocracy of the country, his family being of pure Spanish blood, and once of considerable importance in Mexico. His father had been governor of the province, and, having amassed a large property, settled at San Diego, where he built a large house with a court-yard in front, kept a retinue of Indians, and set up for the grandee of that part of the country. His son was sent to Mexico, where he received an education, and went into the first society of the capital. Misfortune, extravagance, and the want of any manner of getting interest on money, soon ate the estate up, and Don Juan Bandini returned from Mexico accomplished, poor, and proud, and without any office or occupation, to lead the life of most young men of the better families, — dissipated and extravagant when the means are at hand; ambitious at heart, and impotent in act; often pinched for bread; keeping up an appearance of style, when their poverty is known to each half-naked Indian boy in the street, and standing in dread of every small trader and shopkeeper in the place. He had a slight and elegant figure, moved gracefully, danced and waltzed beautifully, spoke good Castilian, with a pleasant and refined voice and accent, and had, throughout, the bearing of a man of birth and figure. Yet here he was, with his passage given him (as I afterwards learned), for he had not the means of paying for it, and living upon the charity of our agent. He was polite to every one,

[9] *Gil Blas* is an eighteenth-century French novel, set in Spain, which features the protagonist's observations on different classes of Spanish society.

spoke to the sailors, and gave four reals—I dare say the last he had in his pocket—to the steward, who waited upon him. I could not but feel a pity for him, especially when I saw him by the side of his fellow-passenger and townsman, a fat, coarse, vulgar, pretentious fellow of a Yankee trader, who had made money in San Diego, and was eating out the vitals of the Bandinis, fattening upon their extravagance, grinding them in their poverty; having mortgages on their lands, forestalling their cattle, and already making an inroad upon their jewels, which were their last hope.

19

EDWIN BRYANT

What I Saw in California

1848

Bryant, a cousin of the poet William Cullen Bryant, was born in Pelham, Massachusetts, in 1805. He edited and published a series of newspapers in Providence, Rhode Island; Rochester, New York; and Louisville and Lexington, Kentucky. In Kentucky his newspapers were highly partisan pro-Whig publications that indulged nativist and anti-Catholic sentiments. In 1846, Bryant joined an overland expedition to California. He was one of the emigrant party who, concerned about the slow pace of the larger group, went on ahead to California. Part of the group that he left behind—the infamous Donner party—was stranded in the Sierra Nevada in the winter of 1846–1847 and, facing starvation, resorted to cannibalism. Bryant served with John Frémont in the Bear Flag Rebellion, and was later appointed alcalde (mayor) of San Francisco. In that capacity, he acquired a number of valuable city lots—an investment that made him wealthy. He returned east in 1847. His account of California, published in 1848, was widely read by California emigrants.

[August 31, 1846] Crossing the Rio de los Americanos, the waters of which, at this season, are quite shallow at the ford, we proceeded over a well-beaten road to Sutter's Fort, arriving there when the sun was about

Edwin Bryant, *What I Saw in California, 1848* (Lincoln: University of Nebraska Press, 1985), 246–47, 266–69.

an hour and a half high. Riding up to the front gate I saw two Indian senti-
nels pacing to and fro before it, and several Americans, or *foreigners* (as all
who are not Californians by birth are here called), sitting in the gateway,
dressed in buckskins and pantaloons and blue sailors' shirts with white
stars worked on the collars. I inquired if Captain Sutter was in the fort?
A very small man, with a peculiarly red face and a most voluble tongue,
gave the response. He was probably a corporal. He said in substance, that
perhaps I was not aware of the great changes which had recently taken
place in California; that the fort now belonged to the United States, and
that Captain Sutter, although he was in the fort, had no control over it. ...

[September 3] Captain Sutter received us with manifestations of cordial hospitality. He is a gentleman between forty-five and fifty years of age,
and in manners, dress, and general deportment, he approaches so near
what we call the "old school gentleman" as to present a gulfy contrast from
the rude society by which he is surrounded. Captain Sutter is a native of
Switzerland, and was at one time an officer in the French army. He emigrated to the United States, and was naturalized. From thence, after a series
of most extraordinary and romantic incidents, to relate which would furnish matter for a volume, he planted himself on the spot where his fort now
stands, then a savage wilderness, and in the midst of numerous and hostile
tribes of Indians. With the small party of men which he originally brought
with him, he succeeded in defending himself against the Indians. ... He
succeeded by degrees in reducing the Indians to obedience, and by means
of their labor erected the spacious fortification which now belongs to him.

The fort is a parallelogram, about five hundred feet in length and
one hundred and fifty in breadth. The walls are constructed of adobes,
or sun-dried bricks. The main building, or residence, stands near the
centre of the area, or court, enclosed by the walls. A row of shops, store-
rooms, and barracks, are enclosed within, and line the walls on every
side. Bastions project from the angles, the ordnance mounted in which
sweep the walls. The principal gates on the wast and south are also
defended by heavy artillery, through portholes pierced in the walls. At
this time the fort is manned by about fifty well-disciplined Indians, and
ten or twelve white men, all under the employ of the United States. ...

The number of laboring Indians employed by Captain Sutter during
the seasons of sowing and harvest is from two to three hundred. Some
of these are clothed in shirts and blankets, but a large portion of them
are entirely naked. They are paid so much per day for their labor, in
such articles of merchandise as they may select from the store. Cotton
cloth and handkerchiefs are what they most freely purchase. Common
brown cloth sells at one dollar per yard. A tin coin issued by Captain

Sutter circulates among them, upon which is stamped the number of days that the holder has laborerd. These stamps indicate the value in merchandise to which the laborer or holder is entitled. ...

The laboring or field Indians about the fort are fed upon the offal of slaughtered animals, and upon the bran sifted from the ground wheat. That is boiled in large iron kettles. It is then placed in wooden troughs standing in the court, around which the several messes seat themselves and scoop out with their hands this poor fodder. Bad as it is, they eat it with an apparent high relish; and no doubt it is more palatable and more healthy than the acorn, mush, or *atóle*, which constitutes the principal food of these Indians in their wild state.

The wheat crop of Captain Sutter, the present year (1846), is about eight thousand bushels. ... Wheat is selling at the fort at two dollars and fifty cents per fanega, rather more than two bushels English measure. It brings the same price when delivered at San Francisco. ... The reason of this high price is the scarcity of flouring-mills in this country. ...

20

JOHN S. HITTELL

Mexican Land-Claims in California

April 1858

Hittell was born in Jonestown, Pennsylvania, in 1825, and studied at Miami University in Oxford, Ohio. He came to California in 1849 and eventually became an editor of the San Francisco newspaper, the Daily Alta California.

The establishment of the American dominion in California, made it necessary that the titles to land, owned in the State, under grants from Mexico, should be recognized and protected in accordance with the principles of American law. Protection was due to the land owners under the general principles of equity and the laws of nations, and had been

John S. Hittell, "Mexican Land-Claims in California," *Hutchings California Magazine* (April 1858).

expressly provided in the treaty of Guadalupe Hidalgo. It was necessary that the protection should be in accordance with the principles of American law, because the vast majority of the population soon came to be composed of Americans, who naturally introduced their own system of law, — the only system suited to their method of conducting business.

But there was a question of much difficulty as to how this protection should be furnished. The Mexican titles were lacking in many of the conditions necessary to a perfect title under the American laws. The land systems of the two countries were constructed on entirely different principles and with different objects. The Mexican system was a good one for the purposes to be attained by it; it was suited to the wants of the natives of California. They were stockgrowers; — their only occupation, and wealth and staple food was furnished by their herds. They owned immense numbers of horses and horned cattle, and to furnish them with pasture, each ranchero required a large tract of land, which might be used by his own stock, exclusively. The public land in California was very extensive; it was worth nothing; there was little demand for it; no evils had been experienced, none were feared from the accumulation of great tracts, in the hands of a few owners; every grant was supposed to be a benefit to the State, by furnishing a home to a new citizen; and so, large grants were made without stint, on nearly every application. If the applicant could show that the land was public property, and unoccupied, he could obtain from 10,000 to 50,000 acres without expense, on condition that he would make the ranch his home, build a house on it, and place several hundred head of horned cattle upon it. These grants were usually made without any accurate description of the land; there never had been any government survey of any portion of the territory; there were no surveyors in the country to locate the boundaries; neither would the applicants have been willing in most cases to pay for surveys; nor was there any apparent need for them, land being very cheap and quarrels about boundaries very rare. Sometimes the land granted was described with certain fixed natural boundaries. In other cases, the grant might be described as lying in a narrow valley, between two ranges of mountains, and extending from a tree, rock, or clump of willows, up or down the valley far enough to include three, six, or ten square leagues. The most common form of grant was for a certain number of square leagues, lying in a much larger district, bounded by well known land-marks. Thus the famous Mariposa grant of Fremont is for ten square leagues 11,386 acres, equivalent to a tract about nine miles square-in the district bounded by the San Joaquín river on the west, the Sierra Nevada mountains on the east, the Merced river on the north, and the Chowchillas on the south; which district includes nearly 100 square leagues. Under such a grant, the Mexican law allowed the grantee to select any place, within the larger limits, and make it his home.

The grants made were not carefully registered. The law prescribed that the petitions for land should all be preserved, and a record of them kept, and that a registry should be made of all the lands granted; but the affairs of the Governor's office were loosely conducted; and in many cases where the claimants have been in possession for twenty years, and have an undoubted title, there is nothing in the archives or records of the former government to show for it. In many respects the California governor had been very careless about granting lands. Some times they would grant the same lands to several persons; and there was one instance wherein Gov. Micheltorena ordered that every person in the northern District of California, who had petitioned for land before a certain date, and whose petition had not been acted upon, should be the owner of the land asked for; provided the nearest Alcalde should certify that it belonged to the public domain. In these cases no title to the grantees was ever made by the Governor.

I have thus briefly mentioned the main peculiarities of the Mexican system of disposing of the public land in California, as distinguished from the American system. The Mexican government made no survey of the land; granted it away in immense tracts without any fixed boundaries, leaving the grantee a wide discretion in regard to location, and keeping no careful registry of the grants.

When the great immigration of '49 filled the land with Americans, it became necessary to provide for the recognition and protection of the good Mexican titles by the American Courts. But how was this to be done? By the ordinary State Courts? The judges would not be sufficiently able, and would be ignorant of the laws under which the grants had been made; and the juries would be composed of Americans whose interests would lead them to do injustice to the large land-owners. Besides, the lawmakers and judges elected by a deeply interested populace could not be depended upon to do justice under such circumstances.

Or should the protection be rendered by the appointment of a commission, instructed to make a summary examination of all claims, declare all those valid which had been in possession previous to the conquest, and of which some record might be found in the archives; leaving the other claims to be tried in the U.S. Courts? This was the policy which should have been pursued.

But that plan was not to prevail. ... [The] bill "to ascertain and settle the private land claims in the State of California" ... provided that the owners of land should sue the Government or lose their land. But why be subjected to so severe a condition? The land owners had committed no offence, that they should be threatened with spoliation. It was not their fault that the Mexican land system differed from the American. The introduction of a new system by the Government did not justify the invalidation of titles, which had been good before, and the subjection of the owners to tedious and expensive litigation. When the American Government took California, it was in honor bound to leave the titles to property as secure as they were at the time of the transfer, and express provision to this effect was made in the treaty. ...

The Land Commission was opened in this city, January 1st, 1852, and in the ensuing fourteen months, 812 suits were brought, and these were all decided previous to the 3d of March, 1855, at which time the Commission dissolved.

It was severe hardship for owners of land under grants from Mexico, that they should be required to sue the government of the United States (which ought to have protected—not persecuted them) or lose their land; but this hardship was rendered much more severe by the peculiar circumstances under which the suits had to be tried. The trials were to be had in San Francisco at a time when the expenses of traveling and of living in San Francisco were very great, and the fees of lawyers enormous. The prosecution of the suits required a study of the laws of Mexico, in regard to the disposition of the public lands, and this study had, of course, to be paid for by the clients. In many cases the claimants had to come to San Francisco from remote parts of the State; having three hundred miles to travel, bringing their witnesses with them at their own expense. The witnesses were nearly all native Californians, and it was necessary to employ interpreters at high prices.

Meanwhile the claimant could not dispose of his land, on account of the cloud there was on his title: neither could he have it surveyed by the U.S. Surveyor so as to give notice to the public where his land really lay. As he could not give a secure title, nor, in most cases, tell where his boundaries were, the Americans were not disposed to buy the land. Many squatters were, no doubt, glad of a pretext under which they might take other people's land and use it without paying rent; but the circumstances were often such that they were justified in refusing to buy. The number of settlers or squatters became large; they formed a decided majority of the voters in several of the counties; their political influence was great; politicians bowed down before them; all political parties courted them; and most of the U.S. Land Agents, and District Attorneys, appointed under the influence of the California Congressmen, became the representatives of the settler interest, and failed to represent the true interest of the United States. Every device known to the law was resorted to defeat the claimant, or delay the confirmation of his grant, as though it were the interest of the Federal Government to defeat every claimant, or to postpone his success as long as possible.

Eight hundred and twelve important suits, to be tried according to the principles of strange laws, and on evidence given in a strange tongue, and where the testimony, in many of the cases, covered hundreds of pages of manuscript, were not to be disposed of in any brief period. In fact, the Commission did not clear its docket until more than three years after its organization. This delay, which would have been disastrous in any country, was doubly so in California. During the greater portion of this time, the titles to most of the good farming land in the settled districts of the State, were declared to be unsettled. The delay was an encouragement to dishonest, and often a justification of honest squatters. They wanted to cultivate the ground; they could not learn whether the land they wished to occupy, was public or private property; they knew the question would not be decided soon, and therefore they might know, if dishonest, that they might make a profit by seizing land which they were morally certain would be, and should be, confirmed to the claimant; and if honest, they could not be expected to pay for property, to which, in many cases, the title was one in which they could place no confidence. The consequence of the system was, that a large portion of the most valuable farming land in the State was occupied by squatters. This occupation contributed greatly to injure the value of the property. The land owner could not sell his land, nor use it, and yet he was compelled to pay taxes. His ranch brought serious evils upon him. It was the seat of a multitude of squatters, who-as a necessary consequence of antagonistic pecuniary interest, — were his bitter enemies. Cases we know, where they fenced in his best land; laid their claims between his house and his garden; threatened to shoot him if he should trespass on their inclosure; killed his cattle if they broke through the sham fences; cut down his valuable shade and fruit trees, and sold them for fire-wood; made no permanent improvements, and acted generally as tho' they were determined to make all the immediate profit possible, out of the ranch. Such things were not rare: they are familiar to every person who knows the general course of events during the last five years in Sonoma, Solano, Contra Costa, Santa Clara, Santa Cruz and Monterey Counties. Blood was not unfrequently spilled in consequence of the feuds between the land holders and the squatters; the victims in nearly every case, belonging to the former class.

After the Federal Government had committed the error of compelling every Californian land owner to bring suit for his own land, which he had held in indisputable ownership under the Mexican dominion, and even before the independence of Mexico and Spain, and after the Government stubbornly contested every case before a tribunal whose learning, ability, and honesty, was and is, universally admitted, — after all this, it is strange that those persons, whose claims were confirmed, and who had been in possession of their land before the American conquest, and in cases where there was no suspicion of fraud, were not allowed to take their own property once for all. But no; Uncle Sam told all the Californians who had gained their suits, that they should not take their land till they had sued him again; he would appeal every case; the claimant must make another fight for his property, or be despoiled.

Here, then, was the whole work to be gone over again in the Federal District Courts, of which there are two in the State; and in each district there are about four hundred claims, to be tried by a judge, much of whose time is occupied with the trial of admiralty cases. The land suits must all be defended, or attended to, by the United States District Attorney, much of whose time is occupied with criminal cases, and civil business in which the Federal Government is interested. The result is delay upon delay. ...

Only two pleas have been made to extenuate or justify the stubborn opposition made by the agents of the Government to the recognition of the Californian land holders. These pleas are, first, that many of the claims are fraudulent; and, secondly, that the Californians claim too much land.

It is not true that many of the claims are fraudulent. The Land Commission did not reject one claim, and the District Courts have rejected only two, on the ground of fraud. There may be twenty-five fraudulent claims in all; I believe not more. There may be many claims which would not have been valid under the Mexican law; but these are not fraudulent, and have been, or will be rejected. But even if there were a hundred, that would be no reason why the Government should attempt to rob the holders of land under titles undoubtedly good in equity and under the Mexican law. A distinction might be made between the two classes, of the suspicious and the undoubtedly good claims. But the Federal Government made no distinction. The Peralta grant, which was made in the last century, and has been in constant possession ever since, under a perfect title according to the Mexican law, was subjected to the same litigation and vexacious delay, and was given over to the tender mercies of the squatters in the same manner with the most questionable title in all the land.

The other plea is still worse. It may be that the welfare of the people requires the land to be equally divided among them; but shall that justify the Government in robbing—directly by violence, or indirectly by litigation—the owners of large tracts? If it be wrong for me to rob my neighbor of his dollars, is it right for Uncle Sam to rob Peralta, or any other Californian, of his land? ... I admit that it were far better for the country that the Mexican grant-holders should not own so much land; I admit that it were better, looking at the question abstractly, that the settlers are more active and industrious, and contribute vastly more, in proportion to their means, to the development and wealth of the State, than do the native holders of the large grants; but all this has nothing to do with the main question.

The question now naturally arises, whether, a great wrong having been done, there is no remedy? Are not the sufferers entitled to an indemnity from Congress?

...Not only has the system adopted by the Federal Government, in regard to Mexican grants, been most injurious and unjust to the claimants, but it has also been very injurious to the country at large. It has deprived the people in the most populous agricultural districts, of permanent titles; has prevented the erection of fine houses, valuable improvements, permanent homes; has contributed to make the population unsettled; to keep families from coming to the country; and, in fine, has been one of the chief causes of the present unsound condition of the social and business relations of California.

21

CAVE JOHNSON COUTS, ABEL STEARNS, AND CHARLES JOHNSON

Letters

1852–1857

Couts, Stearns, and Johnson were brothers-in-law, born in the United States (Couts in Tennessee, Stearns and Johnson in Massachusetts), who each married one of the five daughters of the southern California ranchero Juan Bandini. Stearns was born in Massachusetts in 1798, went to sea as a twelve-year-old orphan, made a large fortune as a

Letters of Cave Johnson Couts, Abel Stearns, and Charles Johnson, Cave Johnson Couts Collection and Abel Stearns Collection, Huntington Library.

merchant, and in 1829 established a business dealing in hides and tallow in San Pedro. He plowed the profits of his commercial dealings into land: by the time of the Gold Rush, he owned 450,000 acres in southern California. He also married into Californio society: In 1841, he married thirteen-year-old Arcadia Bandini. Johnson was born in Marblehead, Massachusetts, in 1830; he first came to California as a merchant seaman in 1847. He married Dolores Bandini in 1851. He was the nephew of Alfred Robinson, another Yankee merchant who had married into the de la Guerra ranchero family of Santa Barbara. Couts was born in Springfield, Tennessee, graduated from West Point in 1843, and came to California in 1849 as a lieutenant in the 1st U.S. Dragoons, following the Mexican-American War. He married Ysidora Bandini in 1851. By marrying his daughters to Americans (two of whom were successful merchants), Bandini brought an infusion of capital into his land- and cattle-rich but cash-poor rancheros. As the United States Land Commission began its work reviewing Mexican land grants, Bandini also understood that Americans had better standing in U.S. courtrooms. For their part, Couts, Stearns, and Johnson saw the Gold Rush as an opportunity to shift away from the hide and tallow trade to the much more lucrative business of supplying beef to the gold country. Alas, moderate droughts in the late 1850s only presaged disastrous droughts in 1863–1864. Johnson returned to being a seagoing merchant; Couts became a sheep-raiser; and Stearns, having sold most of his lands to cover his debts, dealt what few lands remained to him to developers.

Johnson, San Diego, to Stearns, May 26, 1851

On the 18th of December 1850, Don Juan borrowed of Adolfo Savin (a frenchman, gambler, &c.) of this place, the sum of $10,800, giving his note payable on the 28th of February, which note he was not able to meet, when they made an arrangement to let the note run on 4% a month interest; in the month of April Don Adolfo asked for a mortgage which Don Juan gave him, on the hotel he built and the old family house on the Plaza; the mortgage is for $12,822.90, the amt of the note with interest up to the first of July, when if not paid the mortgage will be closed, and the property sacrificed. When Don Juan left here for the rancho[10] it was his intention to put sufficient Cattle on the road, to meet the payments; he arrived there and found everything in a bad state, nothing planted, and his cattle here, there, and everywhere. ...

[10] At Guadalupe, Baja California.

Johnson, Santo Tomás,[11] to Stearns, January 27, 1852

I have received very bad accounts of your Cattle at San Rafael, it has only rained once here, and then very little, of course there is no grass; your cattle are so poor and weak they can hardly move, and undoubtedly you have lost a good many; the Cattle in "Guadalupe" are in the same condition, and if we have no more rain, we shall lose full one half of them.

Couts, San Pedro, to Stearns, August 14, 1852

I sold out on 24 last month, delivered my whole stock at San Joaquin City (opposite mouth of Stanislaus) at $20 per head, delivered 943 head—big and little. Considering the number of calves and colts, think I made the best sale of any one that I know of, particularly as many of my cows were *most ordinary*. I will be in Los Angeles in the course of a couple of weeks, and if we can make an arrangement, will go up again with cattle.

Johnson, San Diego, to Stearns, November 11, 1852

Don Juan has a strong idea of driving up 1000 head of cattle in March; in my opinion that is very foolish, as his *stumpy cows* won't bring enough to pay for the trouble of driving them; he has the proof of that by experience.

Johnson, San Francisco, to Stearns, June 7, 1853

[A]s long as we keep our liabilities amongst ourselves, we understand each other, and always know "how" we stand.

Stearns, Los Angeles, to Andrew Randall, October 14, 1853

I have, in all, some 20,000 head of Stock to be taken care of. ... [W]e find a ready Market or Sale for our Cattle without the risk and expense of driving them. Cattle in this Section of the State are on the decrease, so much so, that our grasiers in this country will have disposed of (this year) some fifteen thousand more than the increase. ... I am happy to learn that you have become an Extensive Grasier and hope you will be successful in your undertaking. Such is our fate, that we have the most enemies of any persons in the Country. Horse stealing and Bullock stealing is the order of the day—and if we don't furnish the Epicures with fatback they curse us—"besides" a suit at law with the govt to see which of Squatters' rights shall be owners of our lands. ...

[11] Baja California.

Stearns, Los Angeles, to Couts, March 26, 1854

It appears you are surrounded by Squatters but I believe by a very good class and presume they will not intrude on you.

Stearns, Los Angeles, to Couts, April 7, 1857

[Your letter] gives rather deplorable condition of the state of the pasture in your Section, and it is equally as bad here even from Santa Barbara down. My ranchos here are much worse than last year. You will most likely have to drive your cattle to the North at least such as you intend selling, as the purchasers here have been buying small lots of cattle at very low prices. ... In case you have to drive I shall probably want to send the larger part of my cattle at your place. José Ma gives me a bad account of the pasture at San Rafael. I shall have all the novillas at that place "from" one year old up taken out. I have bad accounts also from Temecula and shall probably have to move the cattle from there. ... Yesterday Julian Charles ... sold all his stock, large and small at 12$ per head, all that have the iron, about 1000 head this year calves not counted. Perhaps there may be some more purchasers down by the Steamer. ... The price you mention 2 year old and up @ 15$ is low still under the present circumstances, perhaps it would be better to sell at that, than to drive. Should you drive to the north, you must calculate on eight or ten months delay to get a good price for your cattle.

22

JUAN BANDINI

Last Will and Testament

1859

Bandini was born in Lima, Peru, in 1800, the son of a successful Spanish merchant. He came to California in 1819. In 1831, he was one of a group of Californios who advocated for the removal of a conservative provincial governor and his replacement with a pro-secularization and pro-development official. In 1833, Bandini served as California's

Last Will and Testament of Juan Bandini (1859), Bancroft Library, University of California at Berkeley.

representative to Mexico City, where he lobbied for secularization
and land reform. He received his first land grant upon his return to
California in 1834. Further grants followed in 1839, 1841, and 1846.
Bandini's efforts to establish profitable ranches ended in failure, however,
even before the distastrous droughts of 1863–1864, and at the time of his
death in 1859 he had already been forced to sell much of his land and still
owed one of his sons-in-law $2,000.

After my death, my Executors will take possession of all my property, give an inventory and a valuation of its intrinsic value, and they shall try to conserve it until the payment of my debts. ...

I am a debtor to Don Abel Stearns, in whose power are my signed notes and besides some $2000.00, more or less. ...

I want my executors as soon as possible to arrange the payments to my creditors so that they are satisfied and in the best harmony with my family, begging them to avoid any kind of trouble or break which may take to poverty my wife and older and younger children, whose only source of income is this small patrimony which I leave them, and which I have been able to keep by dint of much work and economy.

5

Natives

The demographic collapse of California natives was sudden and significant. When the Spanish first arrived in California in 1769, there were perhaps 300,000 natives in California. When the Gold Rush began, there were still 150,000. During the 1850s, the native population fell to 30,000. Disease, famine, and violence were the primary causes of the Indian population collapse. Racist attitudes—ably demonstrated by the Sacramento merchant Isaac Perkins—undergirded the violence. Those attitudes informed a statement of policy written in 1852 by a group of miners in northern California that spelled out the punishment for alleged Indian crimes: the massacre of the native inhabitants of local villages. Stephen Powers described the culture of a native northern California society, the Chi-mal'-a-kwe, who suffered just such a massacre at the hands of miners. Bret Harte described a similar massacre of Wiyots in 1860. As the native population declined, and as opportunities for Indians to subsist through fishing salmon and gathering acorns receded in the face of miners' alterations of the environment, natives were gradually drawn into the wage labor force.

23

ISAAC PERKINS

Letter to Daniel Perkins

January 30, 1851

Perkins was born in Massachusetts in 1816 and came to California in 1850.

Isaac Perkins Correspondence, California State Library.

[Wh]ilst I was at Marysville I visited a 'rancheree' of Digger Indians. You have probably heard something of this class of California natives. ... [A] t this Rancheree there is about two hundred Indians, tha make there huts by making holes in the ground & turf them over leving a round hole in front just big enough to crawl in . ... [Acorns] is pritty much all tha have to live on for tha are to lazy & stupid to catch game of Fish both of which the country abounds, tha are the most stupid set of bens [beings] I ever did see tha lay in the dirt in front of there huts & eat acorns & then croll in there holes. Now I don't wish to say any thing aganst the fair Seck but these Digger women are the fatist nastyest & stupidest set I ever did see. Tha ware but little or no close, it must have been a genrol laying in time for most every one of them had a baby.

24

GEORGE GIBBS, J. A. WHALEY, C. WOODFORD, J. W. HOLT, CHAS. LISCOM, R. WILEY, AND EDW. KINGWOOD

To the Governor of California
June 27, 1852

Gibbs and the others were miners on the Trinity-Klamath river system. In May 1852, they suspected that Karok Indians had killed a miner. They set off to find the killers at a Karok settlement on the Salmon River, but the Karoks insisted that the killer was not a member of the village. The miners then adopted the following code and believed it to be effective, because in June the Karoks, fearing the annihilation of their village, identified the alleged murderers. The Karoks were unable to avoid reprisals, however. When the miners came to collect the murderers, they were told that they had fled. The miners then destroyed two Karok villages, killing one man who was unable to flee.

George Gibbs, J. A. Whaley, C. Woodford, J. W. Holt, Chas. Liscom, R. Wiley, and Edw. Kingwood, "the better regulation of our Indian relations...to prevent hasty and inconsiderate revenge on the one hand, and secure adequate punishment on the other," to the governor of California, June 27, 1852. Indian War Papers, California State Archives, Sacramento. In Albert Hurtado, *Indian Survival on the California Frontier* (New Haven: Yale University Press, 1988), 118–19.

[T]o prevent hasty and inconsiderate revenge on the one hand, and secure adequate punishment on the other. ... That in all cases of crime committed by Indians, unless the party should be taken in the act, no revenge should be allowed until an investigation by the neighborhood should take place; that the delivery of the aggressors should be demanded by the nearest ranches, and after a reasonable time given punishment should be inflicted as follows: for murder by the destruction of the ranch to which the criminal belonged and its inhabitants if known. If not known, by that of those nearest the spot. For theft. By destruction of the ranch or such lighter punishment as should be awarded, but life not to be taken except for stealing horses or in preventing robbery. The punishment of a thief when taken in other cases to be whipping, not to exceed 39 lashes; and cutting the hair. Offenses of whites against Indians, whether by killing without cause, burning ranches or otherwise, to be punished [at] ... the discretion of a jury, as also the sale of firearms and ammunition to the Indians.

25

STEPHEN POWERS

The Chi-mal'-a-kwe

1877

Powers was born in Waterford, Ohio, in 1840, and graduated from the University of Michigan in 1863. He traveled overland to California in 1869—walking the distance, even though the transcontinental railroad had already been completed. In California, as a self-taught ethnographer, he undertook the study of Native American groups.

The Chi-mal'-a-kwe lived on the New River, a tributary of the Trinity, but they are now extinct. When the Americans arrived there were only two families, or about twenty-five persons, on that stream who still spoke

Stephen Powers, "The Chi-mal'-a-kwe," *Tribes of California*, 1877 (Berkeley: University of California Press, 1976), 91–95.

Chimalakwe; all the rest of them used Hupâ. On the Trinity itself, from Burnt Ranch up to the mouth of North Fork, there lived a tribe called the Chim-a-rí-ko ... who spoke the same language as the Chimalakwe, and there are perhaps a half-dozen of them yet living. ...

An early pioneer among them named White states that they were once nearly as numerous as the Hupâ, but the restless aggression and persistency of that sturdy race crushed them utterly out. The Chimalkwe seem to represent the true California Indians, while the Hupâ belong to the Athabascan races; and we behold here one of the last conquests of this northern invasion, whose steady progress southward was checked only by the Americans. As stated above, there were two families of Indians speaking more or less Chimalakwe when the whites arrived; but in fifteen years from that time it has dwindled to a mere category of names, though there were not many of the tribe left to speak either Hupâ or Chimalakwe.

They are a melancholy illustration of the rapidity with which the simple tribes of mountaineers have faded away before the white man, while the more pliant and less heroic lowlanders, conserving their strength through sluggishness, have held on for years. When the serpent of civilization came to them, and they found they were naked, like Adam and Eve in the garden, they made for themselves garments or stole them. Then when there came one of those sweltering days of California the savages chafed themselves, and grew hot in their new clothes, and they stripped them off to the last piece. Besides that, they suddenly changed their diet to a semi-civilized fashion. All these things opened a broad door to quick consumption and other maladies, and the poor wretches went off like leaves on a frosty morning in October. It is related that at one time there were not enough able-bodied Indians in the tribe to dig graves for the dead; and the neighboring whites, to their shame be it recorded, refused to assist them, so that many of them became a prey to the birds and the beasts. So they went like a little wisp of fog, no bigger than a man's hand, on the top of a mountain, when the sun comes up in the morning, and they are all gone.

... In the early days, before the mining operations filled up the Trinity, there was a fall five or six feet high at Big Flat, above which the salmon could not pass. Hence the Wintun living on the upper reaches of the river were not so well provisioned as their down-rover neighbors. In running up the river the salmon would accumulate in great numbers at this obstruction, and the Chimariko used to allow the Patch'-a-we (Wintu) living as far up as North Fork and Cañon Creek to come down in the season and catch all they could carry home.

They occupied a long and narrow canon, which was rich in gold placers and tempting to the *auri sacra fames*[12] of the early miners. The mining necessarily roiled the river, so that the Indians could not see to spear salmon. As a matter of course they protested. The miners replied with insults, if nothing worse. Being deprived of salmon, their staff of life, they stole the miners' pack mules and ate them. The miners made bloody reprisals.

The eloquence of Pú-yel-yal-li, of Big Flat, stirred them up to seek revenge, and thus matters went on from bad to worse until the deep canon of the Trinity was luridly lighted up by the torch of war, and reechoed to horrid war-whoops and the yells of the wounded and dying. In 1863–64 the conflict raged with frightful truculence on either side. The Indians for the nonce got the upper hand. For twenty miles along the river there was scarcely a white family or even a miner left; the trading posts were sacked and burned; the ponderous wheels in the bed of the river lazily flapped in the waters now muddied no longer, silent and untended amid the blackened ruins; and the miners' cabins were very small heaps of ashes.

But the Americans finally rallied and returned, and sternly were the Indians taught that they must not presume to discuss with American miners the question of the proper color for the water in Trinity River. They were hunted to the death, shot down one by one, massacred in groups, driven over precipices; but in the bloody business of their taking-off they also dragged down to death with them a great share of the original settlers, who alone could have given some information touching their customs. In the summer of 1871 it was commonly said that there was not an Indian left. The gold was gone too, and the miners for the greater part; and amid the stupendous ripping-up and wreck of the earth which miners leave behind them, in this grim and rock-bound canon, doubly lonesome now with its deserted villages sagging this way and that on little margins of shores, the stripped and rib-smashed cabins, corrugated gravel-beds, shattered turbine-wheels, and the hollow roaring of the river amid the gray bowlders, as if in a kind of querulous lament over its departed glories—long ago, the dark-skinned fishermen peering keenly down from their leafy booths, with spears ready poised; afterward, the restless, toiling bands of miners—one finds himself indulging in this reflection: "The gold is gone, to return no more; the white man wanted nothing else; the Trinity now has nothing but its salmon to offer; the Indian wanted nothing else; would not a tribe of savages be better than this utter and irreclaimable waste, even if the gold had never been gotten?"

---

[12] *auri sacra fames* (Latin), "the cursed hunger for gold."

26

BRET HARTE

Indiscriminate Massacre of Indians: Women and Children Butchered

February 29, 1860

Harte, born Francis Brett Hart in Albany, New York, in 1836, traveled to California in 1853. He eventually found work as a journalist. He published his account of the killing of the Wiyots on Indian Island in the Northern Californian in 1860 when his editor was absent, leaving Harte temporarily in charge.

Our Indian troubles have reached a crisis. Today we record acts of Indian aggression and white retaliation. It is a humiliating fact that the parties who may be supposed to represent white civilization have committed the greater barbarity. But before we review the causes that have led to this crowning act of reckless desperation, let us remind the public at a distance from this savage-ridden district, that the secrecy of this indiscriminate massacre is an evidence of its disavowal and detestation of the community. The perpetrators are yet unknown.

The people of this county have been long-suffering and patient. They have had homes plundered, property destroyed, and the lives of friends sacrificed. The protection of a Federal force has been found inadequate and when volunteer forces have been raised and the captured savages placed on reservations, by some defective screw in the Federal machinery, they have escaped. They have returned to their old homes. Old outrages have been renewed. The friendly Indians about the Bay have been charged with conveying arms and ammunition to the mountain tribes and receiving slaughtered beef as a reward. A class of hard-working men who derive their subsistence by cattle raising have been the greatest sufferers, and if in the blind fury of retaliation they spare neither age or sex, though they cannot be excused a part of the blame should fall upon that government which places the responsibility of self-defense

Bret Harte, "Indiscriminate Massacre of Indians: Women and Children Butchered," *The Northern Californian* (February 29, 1860).

on the injured party. If your government says, virtually, 'Protect yourselves,' it cannot consistently find fault with the manner.

Justice demands that we should show thus much in explanation. We do not extenuate. If the deed was committed by responsible parties, we will give place to any argument that may be offered in justification. But we can conceive of no palliation for woman and child slaughter. We can conceive of no wrong that a babe's blood can atone for. Perhaps we do not rightly understand the doctrine of 'extermination.' How a human being, with the faculty of memory, who could recall his own mother's gray hairs, who could remember how he had been taught to respect age and decrepitude, who had ever looked upon a helpless infant with a father's eye—could with cruel, unpitying hand carry out the 'extermination' that his brain had conceived—who could smite the mother and a child so wantonly and cruelly—few men can understand. What amount of suffering it takes to make a man a babe-killer, is a question for future moralists. What will justify it, should be a question of present law.

It is the 'beginning of the end.' It will not be strange if these separate tribes are gathered into a burning focus on every trail. It will not be safe for the white man to travel alone. Every tree may hide some wretched and revengeful father. A spirit has been raised that nothing but blood will appease. An 'irrepressible conflict' is really here. Knowing this, was it policy to commence the work of extermination with the most peaceful? And what assistance can be expected from a Legislature already perplexed with doubts and suspicion, in the face of the bloody record we today publish?

A report was brought from Eureka on Sunday morning, that during the night nearly all the Indians camping on Indian Island, including women and children, were killed by parties unknown. A few loaded canoes bringing the dead bodies to Union on their way to Mad river, where some of the victims belonged, confirmed the report. But when the facts were generally known, it appeared that out of some sixty or seventy killed on the Island, at least fifty or sixty were women and children. Neither age or sex had been spared. Little children and old women were mercilessly stabbed and their skulls crushed with axes. When the bodies were landed at Union, a more shocking and revolting spectacle never was exhibited to the eyes of a Christian and civilized people. Old women, wrinkled and decrepit, lay weltering in blood, their brains dashed out and dabbled with their long gray hair. Infants scarce a span long, with their faces cloven with hatchets and their bodies ghastly with wounds. We gathered from the survivors that four or five white men attacked the ranches at about 4 o'clock in the morning, which statement is corroborated by people at Eureka who heard pistol shots at about that time, although no knowledge of the attack was public. With the Indians who lived on the Island, some thirty from the mouth of Mad river were staying, having attended a dance on the evening previous. They were all killed with the exception of some few who hid themselves during the massacre. No resistance was made, it is said, to the butchers who did the work, but as they ran or huddled together for protection like sheep, they were struck down with hatchets. Very little shooting was done, most of the bodies having wounds about the head. The bucks were mostly absent, which accounts for the predominance of female victims.

On Monday we received a statement from our Senior, at Eureka en route for San Francisco. He says: 'About 9 o'clock, I visited the Island, and there a horrible scene was presented. The bodies of 36 women and children, recently killed, lay in and near the several ranches—they were of all ages, from the child of but two or three years to the old skeleton squaw. From appearances, the most of them must have been killed with axes or hatchets—at the heads and bodies of many were gashed as with such an instrument. It was a sickening and pitiful sight. Some 5 or 6 were still alive and one old woman was able to talk, although dreadfully wounded. Dr. Lee, who visited them and dressed the wounds of those live, says that some will recover if properly cared for.' It is not generally known that more than three bucks were killed—though it is supposed there must have been 15 or 20. It is thought that the bodies of the men were taken away by Indians early this morning as four canoes were seen to leave the Island.

On the beach south of the entrance it is reported that from thirty to fifty were killed. It is also reported, that at Bucksport, all were killed that were there. I passed in sight of them about 11 o'clock and saw the ranches on fire. It is also said that the same has been done at the several ranches on Eel river.

No one seems to know who was engaged in this slaughter, but is supposed to have been men who have suffered from depredations so long on Eel river and vicinity. It is said that some jerked beef, about 100 lb., was found in one of the Indian ranches on Indian Island and on south beach. Indian Island is scarcely one mile from Eureka, the county seat of Humboldt county. With the exception of the conjectures that the Indians on the Island offer aid and assistance to the mountain Indians, they are peaceful and industrious, and seem to have perfect faith in the good will of the whites. Many of them are familiar to our citizens. 'Bill' of Mad river, a well known and rather intelligent fellow, has proven a faithful ally to the white men on several occasions and—has had his wife, mother, sister, two brothers and two little children, cruelly butchered by men of that race whom he had learned to respect and esteem.

Some of the victims lived a few hours after having been brought up to Union. A number of citizens visited the scene where the canoes were unloaded; and it is but justice to the community and simple humanity to say, that the general expression was one of deep sympathy with the miserable sufferers, and honest, deep and utter abhorrence of the act of wanton brutality, and its perpetrators.

6

Chinese

The demand for labor, filled in part by natives, attracted tens of thousands of Chinese immigrants to California. By 1852, John Bigler, the governor of the state, called for an end to Chinese immigration; Norman Asing, a Chinese immigrant, composed a persuasive rebuttal. Anti-Chinese feelings did not abate, however, as the formation of the "Anti-Coolie Assocation" in 1862 in Humboldt, California, demonstrated. Anti-Chinese nativism eventually resulted in the federal Chinese Exclusion Act in 1882, banning further Chinese migration to the United States and prohibiting Chinese already settled from becoming United States citizens.

27

NORMAN ASING (SANG YUEN)

To His Excellency Gov. Bigler

May 5, 1852

Asing was a San Francisco restaurateur and leader of the Chinese-American community. He was born in the Pearl River delta in the late-eighteenth or early-nineteenth century. He left China around 1820 and lived in New York City and Charlestown, South Carolina, before coming to California in 1849.

Sir: I am a Chinaman, a republican, and a lover of free institutions; am much attached to the principles of the government of the United States,

Norman Asing (Sang Yuen), "To His Excellency Gov. Bigler," *Alta California*, May 5, 1852.

and therefore take the liberty of addressing you as the chief of the government of this State. Your official position gives you a great opportunity of good and evil. Your opinions through a message to a legislative body have weight and, and perhaps none more so with the people, for the effect of your late message has been thus far to prejudice the public mind against my people, to enable those who wait the opportunity to hunt them down, and rob them of the rewards of their toil. You may not have meant that this should be the case, but you can see what will be the result of your propositions.

I am not much acquainted with your logic, that by excluding population from this State you enhance its wealth. I have always considered that population was wealth; particularly a population of producers, of men who by the labor of their hands or intellect, enrich the warehouses or the granaries of the country with the products of nature and art. You are deeply convinced you say "that to enhance the prosperity and preserve the tranquility of this State, Asiatic immigration must be checked." This, your Excellency, is but one step towards a retrograde movement of the government, which, on reflection, you will discover; and which the citizens of this country ought never to tolerate. It was one of the principal causes of quarrel between you (when colonies) and England; when the latter pressed laws against emigration, you looked for immigration; it came, and immigration made you *what you are* — your nation what it is. It transferred you at once from childhood to manhood and made you great and respectable throughout the nations of the earth. I am sure your Excellency cannot, if you would, prevent your being called the descendant of an immigrant, for I am sure you do not boast of being a descendant of the red man. But your further logic is more reprehensible. You argue that this is a republic of a particular race — that the Constitution of the United States admits of no asylum to any other than the pale face. This proposition is false in the extreme, and you know it. The declaration of your independence, and all the acts of your government, your people, and your history are all against you.

It is true, you have degraded the Negro because of your holding him in involuntary servitude, and because for the sake of union in some of your states such was tolerated, and amongst this class you would endeavor to place us; and no doubt it would be pleasing to some would-be freemen to mark the brand of servitude upon us. But we would beg to remind you that when your nation was a wilderness, and the nation from which you sprung barbarous, we exercised most of the arts and virtues of civilized life; that we are possessed of a language and a literature, and that men skilled in science and the arts are numerous among us; that the productions of our manufactories, our sail, and workshops, form no small share of the commerce of the world; and that for centuries, colleges, schools, charitable institutions, asylums, and hospitals, have been as common as in your own land. That our people cannot be reproved for their idleness, and that your historians have given them due credit for the variety and richness of their works of art, and for their simplicity of manners, and particularly their industry. And we beg to remark, that so far as the history of our race in California goes, it stamps with the test of truth the fact that we are not the degraded race you would make us. We came amongst you as mechanics or traders, and following every honorable business of life. You do not find us pursuing occupations of degrading character, except you consider labor degrading, which I am sure you do not; and if our countrymen save the proceeds of their industry from the tavern and the gambling house to spend it on farms or town lots or on their families, surely you will admit that even these are virtues. You say "you desire to see no change in the generous policy of this government as far as regards Europeans." It is out of your power to say, however, in what way or to whom the doctrines of the Constitution shall apply. You have no more right to propose a measure for checking immigration, than you have the right of sending a message to the Legislature on the subject. As far as regards the color and complexion of our race, we are perfectly aware that our population have been a little more tan than yours.

Your Excellency will discover, however, that we are as much allied to the African race and the red man as you are yourself, and that as far as the aristocracy of skin is concerned, ours might compare with many of the European races; nor do we consider that your Excellency, as a Democrat, will make us believe that the framers of your declaration of rights ever suggested the propriety of establishing an aristocracy of skin. I am a naturalized citizen, your Excellency, of Charleston, South Carolina, and a Christian, too; and so hope you will stand corrected in your assertion "that none of the Asiatic class" as you are pleased to term them, have applied for benefits under our naturalization act. I could point out to you numbers of citizens, all over the whole continent, who have taken advantage of your hospitality and citizenship, and I defy you to say that our race have ever abused that hospitality or forfeited their claim on this or any of the governments of South America, by an infringement on the laws of the countries into which they pass. You find us peculiarly peaceable and orderly. It does not cost your state much for our criminal prosecution. We apply less to your courts for redress, and so far as I know, there are none who are a charge upon the state, as paupers.

You say that "gold, with its talismanic power, has overcome those natural habits of non-intercourse we have exhibited." I ask you, has not gold had the same effect upon your people, and the people of other countries, who have migrated hither? Why, it was gold that filled your country (formerly a desert) with people, filled your harbours with ships and opened our much-coveted trade to the enterprise of your merchants.

You cannot, in the face of facts that stare you in the face, assert that the cupidity of which you speak is ours alone; so that your Excellency will perceive that in this age a change of cupidity would not tell. Thousands of your own citizens come here to dig gold, with the idea of returning as speedily as they can.

We think you are in error, however, in this respect, as many of us, and many more, will acquire a domicile amongst you.

But, for the present, I shall take leave of your Excellency, and shall resume this question upon another occasion which I hope you will take into consideration in a spirit of candor. Your predecessor pursued a different line of conduct towards us, as will appear by reference to his message.

I have the honor to be your Excellency's very obedient servant,
NORMAN ASING

28

HUMBOLDT TIMES

Anti-Coolie Association

January 25, 1862

The Anti-Coolie Association, founded in Humboldt County in 1862, was one of numerous nativist groups in California in the early 1860s.

The evils of importing and fostering a population of Chinamen, incapable of ever becoming citizens, or of adding anything to the permanent prosperity of our State, has attracted the attention of the thinking

"Anti-Coolie Association," *Humboldt Times* (January 25, 1862).

portion of our community for a long time. ... [W]e desire to see the cause of exasperation removed. Every year this matter is delayed, the most oppressive will the evil become. The laboring class of our community will feel this competition with Chinamen sorely. While the Chinaman can never be elevated to be a fit associate for a white man, they may be the means of degrading many white men to be fit associates for Chinamen only.

29

MARK TWAIN

Roughing It

1872

Twain, born Samuel Langhorne Clemens in Florida, Missouri, in 1835, traveled west by stage in 1861 following a brief stint as a volunteer in a Confederate unit. He joined his brother, Orion Clemens, in Nevada, where Orion was secretary to the territorial governor. It was in Virginia City, Nevada, that Clemens first used the pen name "Mark Twain," in a humorous contribution to a local newspaper. He decamped for San Francisco in 1864. Roughing It, *his account of his time in the West, was published in 1872.*

Of course there was a large Chinese population in Virginia [City] — it is the case with every town and city on the Pacific coast. They are a harmless race when white men either let them alone or treat them no worse than dogs; in fact they are almost entirely harmless anyhow, for they seldom think of resenting the vilest insults or the cruelest injuries. They are quiet, peaceable, tractable, free from drunkenness, and they are as industrious as the day is long. A disorderly Chinaman is rare, and a lazy one does not exist. So long as a Chinaman has strength to use his hands he needs no support from anybody; white men often complain of want of work, but a Chinaman offers no such complaint; he always manages

Mark Twain, *Roughing It*, 1872 (New York: Signet, 1962), 291–97.

to find something to do. He is a great convenience to everybody—even to the worst class of white men, for he bears the most of their sins, suffering fines for their petty thefts, imprisonment for their robberies, and death for their murders. Any white man can swear a Chinaman's life away in the courts, but no Chinaman can testify against a white man. Ours is the "land of the free"—nobody denies that—nobody challenges it. [Maybe it is because we won't let other people testify.] As I write, news comes that in broad daylight in San Francisco, some boys have stoned an inoffensive Chinaman to death, and that although a large crowd witnessed the shameful deed, no one interfered.

There are seventy thousand (and possibly one hundred thousand) Chinamen on the Pacific coast. There were about a thousand in Virginia. They were penned into a "Chinese quarter"—a thing which they do not particularly object to, as they are fond of herding together. Their buildings were of wood; usually only one story high, and set thickly together along streets scarcely wide enough for a wagon to pass through. Their quarter was a little removed from the rest of the town. The chief employment of Chinamen in towns is to wash clothing. . . . Their price for washing was $2.50 per dozen—rather cheaper than white people could afford to wash for at that time. A very common sign on the Chinese houses was: "See Yup, Washer and Ironer"; "Hong Wo, Washer"; "Sam Sing & Ah Hop, Washing." The house servants, cooks, etc., in California and Nevada, were chiefly Chinamen. There were few white servants and no Chinawomen so employed. Chinamen make good house servants, being quick, obedient, patient, quick to learn and tirelessly industrious. They do not need to be taught a thing twice, as a general thing. They are imitative. If a Chinaman were to see his master break up a centre table, in a passion, and kindle a fire with it, that Chinaman would be likely to resort to the furniture for fuel forever afterward.

All Chinamen can read, write and cipher with easy facility—pity but all our petted voters could. In California they rent little patches of ground and do a deal of gardening. They will raise surprising crops of vegetables on a sand pile. They waste nothing. What is rubbish to a Christian, a Chinaman carefully preserves and makes useful in one way or another. He gathers up all the old oyster and sardine cans that white people throw away, and procures marketable tin and solder from them by melting. He gathers up old bones and turns them into manure. In California he gets a living out of old mining claims that white men have abandoned as exhausted and worthless—and then the officers come down on him once a month with an exorbitant swindle to which the legislature has given the broad, general name of "foreign" mining tax, but it is usually inflicted on no foreigners but Chinamen. This swindle has in some cases been repeated once or twice on the same victim in the course of the same month—but the public treasury was no additionally enriched by it, probably. ...

They are a kindly disposed, well-meaning race, and are respected and well treated by the upper classes, all over the Pacific coast. No Californian gentleman or lady ever abuses or oppresses a Chinaman, under any circumstances, an explanation that seems to be much needed in the East. Only the scum of the population do it—they and their children; they, and, naturally and consistently, the policemen and politicians, likewise, for these are the dust-licking pimps and slaves of the scum, there as well as elsewhere in America.

30

Chinese Exclusion Act
May 6, 1882

Barring Chinese immigration to the United States was a popular political stance among white voters in California, where dozens of nativist organizations were founded in the 1860s and 1870s. Although an earlier version of the Chinese Exclusion Act was vetoed by President Rutherford Hayes in 1878, this version was signed into law by Chester Arthur in 1882.

An Act to Execute Certain Treaty Stipulations Relating to Chinese

Whereas, in the opinion of the Government of the United States the coming of Chinese laborers to this country endangers the good order of certain localities within the territory thereof: Therefore,

Be it enacted by the Senate and House of Representatives of the United States of America in Congress assembled, That from and after the expiration of ninety days next after the passage of this act, and until

Chinese Exclusion Act, May 6, 1882. Enrolled Acts and Resolutions of Congress, 1789–1996; General Records of the United States Government; Record Group 11; National Archives.

the expiration of ten years next after the passage of this act, the coming of Chinese laborers to the United States be, and the same is hereby, suspended; and during such suspension it shall not be lawful for any Chinese laborer to come, or having so come after the expiration of said ninety days, to remain within the United States.

SEC. 2. That the master of any vessel who shall knowingly bring within the United States on such vessel, and land or permit to be landed, any Chinese laborer, from any foreign port or place, shall be deemed guilty of a misdemeanor, and on conviction thereof shall be punished by a fine of not more than $500 for each and every such Chinese laborer so brought, and may be also imprisoned for a term not exceeding one year.

SEC. 3. That the two foregoing sections shall not apply to Chinese laborers who were in the United States on the 17th day of November, 1880, or who shall have come into the same before the expiration of ninety days next after the passage of this act. ...

SEC. 13. That this act shall not apply to diplomatic and other officers of the Chinese Government traveling upon the business of that government, whose credentials shall be taken as equivalent to the certificate in this act mentioned, and shall exempt them and their body and household servants from the provisions of this act as to other Chinese persons.

SEC. 14. That hereafter no State court or court of the United States shall admit Chinese to citizenship; and all laws in conflict with this act are hereby repealed.

SEC. 15. That the words "Chinese laborers," wherever used in this act, shall be construed to mean both skilled and unskilled laborers and Chinese employed in mining.

Approved, May 6, 1882.

7

Environment

Panning for gold gave way to the technology of hydraulic mining by the late 1850s, and the effect on the environment was extensively destructive. John Kinkade described the effect of hydraulic mining on the land as early as 1857. In 1863, William Wells described the mercury mines of New Almaden: By that time, California mined not only one-third of the gold but one-third of the mercury in the world, and hydraulic miners used tons of mercury in their sluices. Testimony before a committee of California state legislators by hydraulic mining company representatives, farmers, steamboat operators, and others on the effects of hydraulic mining detailed not only changes to the environment, but miners' justifications for those changes and calls by farmers and others to put a stop to hydraulic mining.

31

JOHN H. EAGLE

To His Wife, Margaret H. Eagle

April 10, 1852

Eagle, a storekeeper, traveled to California via Panama in 1852.

Auburn Ravine, April 10, 1852. California is a most beautiful country. As you travel from Sacramento to Ophir, you can see the tops of the Sierra Nevada Mountains, covered with snow—in depth 30 or forty feet. This

John H. Eagle, to his wife, Margaret H. Eagle, Allegheny, Pennsylvania, April 10, 1852. Huntington Library.

chain of mountains is said to be about four hundred miles in length, and can be seen at a distance of one hundred miles. When the sun shines on them they look like beautiful white clouds. The country around here is delightful; all the different varieties of flowers that the imagination can paint can be seen here, growing wild from the hills, and in the valleys. ...

But it makes a difference in the appearance when this beautiful scenery is cut up and torn up for the purpose of mining. Among the mines is the roughest and most barren looking places a person can conceive of; to see the ground dug up for miles in some places to the depth of twenty or thirty feet, in hills, valleys, Ravines, creeks, etc.

32

JOHN THOMPSON KINKADE

Letters to James Kinkade

1850–1871

Kinkade was born in 1826. He traveled overland to California in 1849, leaving his brother James in Marysville, Ohio.

Middle Fork of the American River. March 21, 1850. [W]e are camped on the above named place for the purpose of turning the water from the channel of the River, to accomplish this we have joined with nine others making 14. ... The raining season is about over which will be hailed with Joy.

September 6, 1850.

Things in California are assuming a different appearance every day, from bad to worse. The emigrants are crowding in very fast and the country is filled to overflowing.

The only chance now to make a raise is in the Rivers and a great many of them are failing. ... In order to turn a River men must expend a great amount of labor say the principle part of the Year without any income. So all the capital they may have collected last year is exhausted by the time they are ready for digging.

John Thompson Kinkade, *Letters to James Kinkade*, Huntington Library.

American River, May 16, 1852. You have probably heard of the Chinese emigration. They have been coming by the ten thousand. ... They subsist on rice and eat it with a sharp stick.

Indian Valley, September 7, 1853. [A]s I stop to reflect on the past progress of California, I conclude that a view of the same Answer brief and imperfect may interest you. Five years since and traces of the Anglo-saxon were almost imperceptible. The Indians swarmed throughout the country gaining their subsistence by taking game, feeding on Acorns, Roots, grass &c. The country might have been divided into three divisions. Plains or Valleys Deserts & Wilderness. The valleys were confined to the Rivers bounded by skirts of timber and to the southern portion of the State the valleys produce a scarce growth of inferior timber but always producing a most luxuriant growth of grass and abounding with wild cattle and horses. The Desert is that portion between the valleys and the mountains and are undulating barren plains and become dryed by the scorching rays of the sun to the consistence of soft brick. Yet when they become saturated in the raining season are soft as a mortar bed. The wilderness was the mountainous portion with a growth of Pine Fir and Cedar unsurpassed in the world. But since forty-nine the progress of the Anglo-saxon has been rapidly onward. The valleys where once fed the wild ox now wave in a most luxurious growth of grain. Those barren plains by the introduction of water from the Rivers by means of ditches are either (to the Miner or Agriculturalist) paying a good income. The wild cattle are fast being consumed the Horses subdued the Indians recedeing Cities and Towns Churches and Schools Mills &c. are interspersed throughout every portion like unto other countries of a century's growth. At last but greatest of all is government in Cal. This is our general or State election day.

Secret Ravine, December 28, 1856. The winter thus far has been very dry we have had but light showers and few of them but in the mountain districts has been heavy snows. We do not however now depend so much on the rains. For the principal mining districts are now supplied with water by ditches and canals from the Rivers and Mountain Streams. And mining facilities have been decidedly improved that men seem to make as much as three years since. In fact, improvements of every class in Cal. are almost beyond description. Five or six years ago mining was mostly confined to the Rivers and Ravines. Now the surface of the country is being washed away. Mountains are either washed down or tunneled out. Tunneling is now done by machines for boreing. The hills are washed down by hydraulic or water excavation. Conduct from fifty to seventy-fve inches of water from a ditch graded one in ... to a point from fifty to one hundred feet above the point of operating. Allow that water to fall that distance through a hose and be forced through a one inch nozzle directed to a bank in the same manner that your fire engines are. By this means three men can accomplish as much as twenty with shovels. One to direct the water and two to attend the sluices which are set so as to conduct the water and dirt away as the bank falls. Canvas towns are now only to be read of.

August 15, 1857. [E]verywhere in the Sacramento Valley between the Sierra Nevada and Coast Mountains the vigorous and enterprising population that was to be seen a few years since has disappeared. And in their stead an emaciated careworn people are everywhere to be seen. Those who have sojourned but for a short time have escaped most of the consequences to which the Continued Resident has fallen a victim. Now, this you may think is one of my bitter tyrads. Such is not the case. The effects of this climate and the Slaverish occupation of the Miner is unmistakably stamped on our physical organization. The majority are either Sick, Crippled from Rheumatism, Maimed by Accidents, Blind, or Toothless.

March 3, 1858. The resources of the mines are weakening Rapidly. It is as hard to make five dollars now as twenty in forty-nine. And yet the cost of existing and carrying on an operation is really the same. & why? Because Capitalists control the country and keep up a most unnatural disproportion between Consumption and Production.

Rocklin, June 28, 1871. Mining is no longer generally prosecuted by those having a will to work, but is conducted by the few having capital to invest. All that class of mining that was easily discovered and worked has passed away.

33

SACRAMENTO DAILY UNION

Hydraulic Mining

July 11, 1854

John F. Morse founded the Sacramento Daily Union in March 1851. The newspaper—which touted itself as the first daily newspaper in the West—was an important publication for the gold mining industry. In later years, it published articles by Bret Harte and Mark Twain.

"Hydraulic Mining," *Sacramento Daily Union* (July 11, 1854).

After these immense masses of earth are undermined and brought down by the streams forced from the pipes, those same streams are turned upon the fallen earth, and it melts before them, and is carried away through the sluices with almost as much rapidity as if it were a bank of snow. ... These sluices are often from five hundred to a thousand feet long, and cobble-stones and small boulders when thrown into them go tumbling and rumbling their entire length. ... No such labor-saving power has ever been introduced to assist the miner in his applications. By the use of this immensely powerful agent, millions of tons of auriferous earth in the gold-bearing regions of the State, will, in the course of a few years, be run from the hills in long sluices into the ravines and valleys.

34

WILLIAM WELLS

The Quicksilver Mines of New Almaden, California
June 1863

Wells traveled to California by sea in 1849. A journalist, he accompanied William Walker to Nicaragua in the mid-1850s before returning to California.

From San José to the quicksilver mine of New Almaden is twelve miles. The road winds for that distance through the most fertile part of the valley of Santa Clara, which gradually widens into a verdant plain, richly carpeted with wild flowers, and every foot of it "claimed," fenced, and settled upon by those who have come to California not to "make a pile" and return, but to build up and improve a home. ... The whole valley is occupied by comfortable farmers, who live more in the style of the dairymen of the Genesee Valley in New York than pioneer settlers on the verge of civilization.

The ascent to the range of mountains, on the slope of which the mine is situated, is very gradual—scarcely perceptible. ... Beyond appear the

William Wells, "The Quicksilver Mines of New Almaden, California," *Harper's New Monthly Magazine* (June 1863).

brick buildings of the "works." ... Here also are the furnaces in which the ore is smelted. ...

From the works to the mine the distance is a mile and a half. The road follows the base of the mountain, into which it is cut, winding romantically up a gentle ascent. ...

On our way we met several wagons loaded with the dark red ore, which had been broken into small pieces before being submitted to the works below. Five wagons are kept running without intermission. ...

The main entrance to the mine is a tunnel, commenced in 1850, in a side of the mountain. ... Through this an iron rail track passes, the cars receiving the ore as it is brought upon the backs of carriers (*tanateros*) from the excavations. These cars are calculated to carry about a ton each, and are pushed rapidly in and out by hand.

We enter the car and in a few moments are rumbling along this under-ground railroad, with no sound to break the silence besides the heavy breathing of our human propellers. ... These laborers are all Mexicans, and have generally served a sort of apprenticeship in the silver mines of Spanish America. Soon we reach the terminus of the railroad, and step out upon a damp soil eaten hard by the incessant tramp of ore-carriers. ...

About 300 persons are employed in the mine. The work was formerly given out to them by *empresarios* or "bosses" who took the job to deliver at the mouth of the mine a certain number of tons of ore, and, of course, hired their workmen at the lowest possible wages. The laborers in the mine (*barateros*) are a distincy fraternity from the ore-carriers (*tanateros*). Each have their respective calling, and are not willing nor are they every expected to assume each other's places. The tanateros are the most muscular and the best proportioned of all those engaged in the mine. Long practice has inured them to the labor, and a first-rate man will pack 200 pounds up the escalaras without stopping to rest. This method of raising the ore os preferred to any machinery that has been suggested, as the men supply all that the works can distill. ...

The ore is a native red sulphuret of mercury. ... It has a flat conchoidal fracture, is fine grained, opaque, and has generally a fine adamantine lustre, and a color varying from cochineal to ruby red. ...

The ore, after being thoroughly cleaned and broken to the required size, is wheeled in barrows from the pile where it is deposited, along the tops of the furnaces and turned into the receptacles, which are of uniform capacity and open at the tops. These will contain about seven tons of ore each. After being filled, they are closed hermetically. As the ore becomes sublimated the vapors pass through a series of twelve compartments. … In their passage through these compartments such of the vapors as become condensed flow in the form of quicksilver through the numerous small holes into covered troughs, attached to the outside of the furnaces their entire length. …

Each of these furnaces is provided with a large wooden chimney forty feet in height, and from which there are constantly pouring clouds of arsenical vapors. … The tops of these chimneys are quite coated with cakes of white arsenic. …

As early as 1851—the year following the commencement of the workings—there were obtained 1800 quintals (180,000 pounds) of quicksilver. … [I]n 1853, there were exported from the State 18,800 flasks of quicksilver (of 75 pounds each), of 1,410,000 pounds, valued at $683,189, at the rate of fifty cents per pound. In the following year (1854) the amount had increased to 1,449,000 pounds, valued at the same rate at $724,500; and all this did not include what was used in the State for mining purposes, which, with the incredible growth of the new system of "hydraulic mining," now superseding all others, consumes, it is safe to say, a quarter of the entire product of the New Almaden. …

One of the most curious circumstances connected with the New Almaden mine is the effect produced by the mercurial vapors upon the surrounding vegetation. Despite the lofty chimneys, and the close attention that has been devoted to the secret of effectually condensing the volatile matter, its escape from the chimneys withers all green things around. Every tree on the mountainside above the works is dead. … Cattle, feeding within half a mile of the hacienda sicken, and become salivated; and the use of the waters of a spring rising near the works is guarded against. …

The workmen at the furnaces are particularly subjected to the poisonous fumes. These men are only able to work one week out of four, when they are changed to some other employment, and others take their place for a week. Pale, cadaverous faces and leaden eyes are the consequence of even these short spells; and any length of time continued at this labor effectually shortens life and impregnates the system with mercury. … Probably less mercury escapes from the present works of New Almaden mine than at any other; but even here, to such a degree is the air filled with the volatile poison, that the gold coins and watches on the persons of those engaged about the furnaces become galvanized and turn white. In such an atmosphere, one would seem to inhale death with every respiration.

35

HAMILTON SMITH JR.

Circular Letter to Hydraulic Miners

1876

Smith was born in Louisville, Kentucky, in 1840. He worked as an engineer in Indiana and Kentucky, primarily in railroad construction, before traveling to California where he specialized in hydraulic mining.

San Francisco, July, 1876
Dear Sir,

It has been deemed desirable by several gentlemen in this City, who are largely interested in hydraulic gravel mining in California, than an association should be instituted, composed of members residing in various parts of the State, who are owners either in gravel mines, or of canals for the supply of water to such mines, or of tail sluices: the objects of the proposed association to be the interchange of useful knowledge between the members in everything relating to the art of process of gravel mining, and also for the general purpose of mutual benefit and protection. ...

It is also proposed that the association take upon itself, whenever in the opinion of the Trustees it is deemed just and advisable, the defense or protection of any one of its members who may be legally attacked, and where the point at issue involves some general principle, in which the other members are also interested. In this way, the costly and vexatious expenses of long contested litigation, will be defrayed, not by a single individual or corporation, to whom such legal costs might be absolutely ruinous, but by the whole community of gravel miners, on whose united shoulders the burden will fall, and where it properly belongs.

In any such legal contest, where the defeat of the owner of a claim 40 feet square might most seriously imperil the value of all our gravel mines and water properties, it is most apparent that we should defend our just rights in a united body, and not allow the destruction of a single weak member to result in the destruction of us all. ...

Hamilton Smith Jr., *Circular Letters to Hydraulic Miners,* 1876. Milton Mining and Water Company Records, California State Library.

The following named gentlemen of San Francisco have been designated as temporary Trustees. ... J. P. Pierce, representing Excelsior Water Co...; Egbert Judson, representing Spring Valley Mining and Irrigating Co. and Milton Mining and Water Co.; L.L. Robinson, representing Union Gravel Mining Co.; Thomas Price, representing El Dorado Water and Deep Gravel Mining Co. and Blue Tent Concolidated...; Hamilton Smith Jr., representing North Bloomfield G.M.Co. ...

–Hamilton Smith, Jr., Chairman Temporary Organization

36

APPENDIX TO THE JOURNALS OF THE SENATE AND ASSEMBLY OF THE 22nd SESSION OF THE LEGISLATURE OF THE STATE OF CALIFORNIA

Testimony Taken by the Committee on Mining Debris, as Reported to the Assembly, 22nd Sess.

1877–1878

By 1878, voters concerned about hydraulic mining debris in California's rivers—primarily farmers in the Sacramento Valley—had won a majority of representatives in the state legislature. The majority convened a series of special hearings to look into the debris question.

Testimony at the Office of the Board of State Harbor Commissioners, San Francisco, February 2, 1878

A. T. Arrowsmith: [S]ome two years since I had occasion ... to make some examinations on Bear River and its tributaries, in regard to the amount of mining that was done on that stream. ... I found that the amount of tailings passing the dam of the Bear River Ditch daily, was 29,000 cubic yards, or four and a half million cubic yards per annum.

"Testimony Taken by the Committee on Mining Debris, as Reported to the Assembly," 22nd Sess. 1877–78. *Appendix to the Journals of the Senate and Assembly of the 22nd Session of the Legislature of the State of California* (Sacramento: F. P. Thompson, 1878), 3–158.

Then the amount of debris deposited on the farming lands below Bear River Cañon is estimated at sixty-three and a half million cubic yards, that is to say ... 10,000 acres covered three feet in depth. ... At least 50,000 acres are liable to be injured by this debris.

Mr. Waters: Would any reasonable system of levees prevent this ... ?

Arrowsmith: An idea was suggested for the construction of a canal from the mouth of Bear River Cañon down to the tules, and to have all this debris carried down to the tules and cover them up, but ... no canal of a sufficient grade could be obtained on those level lands there, and ...the canal, like the channel of the river, would fill up just in the same way. ... [T]he original channel, as I recollect it at that early day [1851] ... was, perhaps one hundred and fifty to two hundred feet in width, from surface to surface, and from fifteen to twenty feet in depth. ... Now, it is entirely obliterated. There is probably no channel of Bear River now; the water just spreads itself.

Mr. Garber: Is the land that is covered entirely ruined?

Arrowsmith: Entirely ruined. ... Simply a gravel and sand bank. ...

B. S. Alexander: [D]ebris, from the mines I suppose, has done more or less injury to farming land. ... [S]ediment comes down and is deposited, some of it in the bed of the river, tending to raise the bed, and a great deal in Suisun Bay. ... This is not the only thing that tends to fill up the river bed and these bays. I should think that the increase of agriculture, the plowing up of the land, making it more easy to be washed off, has as much to do with is as the mines. ... I have been up to Stone Creek in a flood on two occasions, way above Jacinto. It is all muddy there in a flood. Now, what does this come from? It is not the mines. There is little mining up there. It comes from the plowing of the land. ...

I don't believe ... that the mining debris that comes down from the mines, which sometimes gets out through the Golden Gate, has anything, and if it has it is very little, to do with the formation of the bar there. I think that the bar is formed entirely, or almost entirely, by the action of the sea—in heavy swells of wind. I am rather of the opinion that the Sacramento River, and if possible the San Joaquin to some extent, the Feather, too, ought to ... [have] banks built on them, high enough and strong enough to keep off any floods—banks like those in Egypt, at the Nile, for instance—they have the same on the Po, too, though I am not so familiar with them—twenty feet high, fifty feet wide, two hundred feet of base—something of that kind—if you could keep all the waters in the rivers; I believe the flood would scour out these bottoms, and we would have navigable rivers.

Testimony at the Office of the Board of State Harbor Commissioners, San Francisco, February 4, 1878

L. L. Robinson: [T]he largest proportion [of gravel], in the shape of boulders and coarse gravel, finds a resting place in either the canons in which the mines discharge their material, or in the beds of the rivers in proximity to the mouth of these tributary canons. By the time debris from the mines reaches the main river, the quantity held in suspense in the water will not amount to three percent of the amount originally moved. And by the time this reaches the lower rivers or bays, where it is finally lodged or deposited, it will not amount to more than two percent of the gravel mined. ... [I]t will only amount per year to six hundred thousand cubic yards—a quantity quite inappreciable in the great mass of material brought into the lower rivers and bays from other causes than hydraulic mining.

...It cannot be denied that much of the largest portion of the immediate damage to the farmers near, or at the mouths of these mining rivers (by covering their lands with 'slickens') is due to mining operations, yet even this is not due to mining alone. The great evil, charged upon hydraulic miners alone, of the filling up of lower rivers, bays, and harbor, arises from two causes, exclusive of their operations. ... These causes are: First, natural ones, and second, principally from the operations of the farmers themselves.

...The destruction of the timber upon the mountain slopes has opened the soil fort the action of the elements; the operations of the agriculturalists in breaking up the surface of the soil has also rendered it more liable to the action of the elements.

...[T]he evils charged upon the miners alone, by the agricultural interests—of filling up the bay and the harbor—really arose in much the larger degree from the agriculturalists themselves.

...[T]he whole of the upper rivers, from the foot of the mountains ... is filling; the whole country is raising—we all know that; that is the law of all alluvial rivers. I have seen it all over the world—the Po, the Rhone, the Rhine. I have seen it in all the rivers. ... Take the rivers in Europe, that we now have thirty and forty feet above the plains; that has not been done by hydraulic mines.

Hamilton Smith, Jr.: My business is that of civil engineer ... and for the last eight or ten years devoted almost exclusively to hydraulic engineering. ... I should estimate that there has been expended of San Francisco capital ... anywhere from 35 to 50 million dollars in these mines. ... [T]hey were certainly worth $100 million. ... The total production of gold from California is between 18 and 19 million dollars a year. That production has been increasing for the last three years, until, I believe, within four or five years, if nothing is done to interfere with mining, the production of the precious metals will amount to as large as 25 million. ... [O]ver a seventh of the entire population of the State reside[s] in those mining counties.

...That the cultivation of the soil will increase the amount of material coming down a river I know from the Ohio River. One hundred years ago the Ohio was one of the most clear and most beautiful streams of anywhere in the world. ... Now ... it is very muddy even at low water. That change is, of course, simply due to cutting the timber away and plowing up the roots, and allowing the cultivation of the ground—disturbing the soil—and the heavy rains wash that into the stream.

Testimony at Marysville, February 16, 1878

W. H. Drum: When I first settled there, we had banks in the Yuba River that were fully twenty-five feet high in low water. As to this filling of the rivers, it has been done within the fifteen years ... I never noticed any perceptible filling previous to the commencement of hydraulic mining. ... It has been filling up more the last ten years; and during the past two years, it has filled more, perhaps, than during the ten preceding years. ... My main land I have not attempted to farm for several years. ... [T]he tract of land I had was worth there, before it was filled up, two hundred thousand dollars. ... They were all alluvial lands, bottom lands, the finiest to be found anywhere. ... I don't think they can be reclaimed. The main bottom is from five to ten feet deep, with sand and sediment. My main bottom lands are covered eight to fifteen feet deep with the stuff. ... [T]here can be but one remedy, in my opinion, and that is to stop the debris from coming.

... [O]n the main surface. Where the telegraph line runs ... I found there was but from four to six feet of the tops of the poles left sticking out. The length of the poles, I believe, is from twenty to twenty-five feet.

Joseph Johnson: [Filling in} commenced in the fall of 1857, from that it increased rapidly on the Yuba and on the Bear River. ... [I]t is caused by the tailings washed down from the mountains by the hydraulic mines. ... When [the tailings] first came down the river you could cultivate the land, but it has got so now you cannot cultivate it or make anything grow on it. ... [T]he channel [of the Yuba River] is filled up and the river runs a mile away from it today. ...

Mr. Kercheval: Now, I understand that the bed of the river, where it is confined within these levees now, is several feet above the lands outside of these levees; that the channel, or bed of the river, is that much higher than the country around. Now, in case it gives way, would these waters not be precipitated all over the country?

Johnson: Most certainly.

George Ohlyer: On the Yuba, aside from these rich farms that have been destroyed, there were immense orchards. ... [T]he Briggs orchard ... was one of the finest orchards in the State, and was entirely destroyed. ... From here down, outside of the limits of the city, there was quite a town, clear down to the Feather River ... fifty or sixty houses. ... All that has been destroyed. ... The Yuba had a channel once, a very deep one. The Feather had a channel once, a very deep one. ... And yet these channels are filled up. Now it is proposed that we levee; that the farmers raise all these levees and preserve these channels. My impression is that these channels will keep filling until you get the whole surrounding country filled. Levees will break. ...

Mr. Dibble: You think it is more impossible for the State of California to restrain these streams than it is for the State of Louisiana to build levees strong enough to restrain and confine the waters of the great Mississippi?

Ohlyer: [T]heir levees are breaking every year or two. ... Why not enact laws regulating mining? ... I don't believe it is right for a miner to use the river for a dump, if he can construct any other place for his tailings. ...

J. H. Jewett: [In 1850] I found the Yuba a bright, clear stream, with pebbly bottom, where you could drive a team across in summer time. There were all kinds of fish in the river. I found some of the most beautiful bottom lands I ever saw. ... All that land ... is now a perfect desert—worth nothing at all. ... As one consequence of the mining debris, in the flood of 1874 the loss of personal property was not less than half a million dollars here. ... Our town was larger in 1853 than it is today.

Testimony at Marysville, February 17, 1878

J. O'Brien: I think if I dumped my tailings directly on your farm and ruined your property that I should be compelled to take care of them; but I am speaking of a case where we dump our tailings into the river twenty miles above, or in some instances one hundred miles above, and it remains there until the storms bring it down here. I don't think we are any more responsible for that than we would be for a landslide in the mountains. ...

Claude Chaney: I live in Wheatland, Yuba County. I came to this country in the fall of 1846. I have lived there pretty near all the time. When I came there these rivers were deep, clear streams. They remained so until

1860. Up at my house, the river was eighteen feet deep and not over one hundred yards wide. At that time I owned a valuable ranch in there. That ranch is now entirely covered up with sand and gravel, entirely destroyed.

Testimony at Sacramento, Feb 1878

J. H. Keyes: In 1856 … [Bear River] was a clear, running stream, with well defined banks, and it remained so until about 1860 or 1861, when it commenced to fill up, and since then it has entirely obliterated the channel, running over the bottom lands in every direction. The fill that has taken place at the mouth of the cañon, on Bear River, is about sixty feet above the level of the channel, and about the confluence of the Bear River with the Feather the fill over the bottom lands is about twelve feet, and the bed of the stream has raised in about the same proportion. …

[I]t comes form the mines entirely. … About the first fill we received down there was a light material, and to a certain extent it was rich. Now the fill is a coarse sand and gravel, and has no productive qualities of its own. I estimate, that the total area of land injured … in the Counties of Yuba, Placer, and Sutter, by reason of this fill, at about 50,000 acres. …

L. F. Moulton: In 1853–54 … the Yuba … was a clear stream, and the banks … were twenty-five feet, at least, above the water. Now they are filled up very much from the mining debris. … I think this poisons the land. … It is like alkali in its effects.

37

Woodruff v. North Bloomfield Gravel Mining Co.
January 7, 1884

Lorenzo Sawyer, the federal judge who ruled in the Woodruff case, was born in Le Roy, New York, in 1820, and studied to become a lawyer in Ohio. In 1850, he traveled overland to California, and eventually opened a law practice in Nevada City. He became a member of the California Supreme Court in 1863, Chief Justice in 1868, and a federal circuit court judge for the Ninth District in 1870.

Woodruff v. North Bloomfield Gravel Mining Company 18 F9 753, January 7, 1884.

The Yuba river rises in the Sierra Nevada mountains, and after flowing in a westerly direction about 12 miles across the plain after leaving the foot-hills, joins the Feather. At the junction, within the angle of these two rivers, is situated the city of Marysville. The Feather thence runs about 30 miles and empties into the Sacramento. These three rivers were originally navigable for steam-boats and other vessels for more than 150 miles from the ocean, at least as far as Marysville — the Sacramento being navigable for the largest-sized steamers. The defendants have for several years been and they are still engaged in hydraulic mining, to a very great extent, in the Sierra Nevada mountains, and have discharged and they are discharging their mining debris, — rocks, pebbles, gravel, and sand, — to a very large amount, into the head-waters of the Yuba, whence it is carried down, by the ordinary current and by floods, into the lower portions of that stream, and into the Feather and the Sacramento. The debris thus discharged has produced the following effects: It has filled up the natural channel of the Yuba above the level of its banks and of the surrounding country, and also of the Feather below the mouth of the Yuba, to the depth of 15 feet or more. It has buried with sand and gravel and destroyed all the farms of the riparian owners on either side of the Yuba, over a space two miles wide and twelve miles long. It is only restrained from working a similar destruction to a much larger extent of farming country on both sides of these rivers, and from in like manner destroying or injuring the city of Marysville, by means of a system of levees, erected at great public expense by the property owners of the county and inhabitants of the city, which levees continually and yearly require to be enlarged and strengthened to keep pace with the increase in the mass of debris thus sent down, at a great annual cost, defrayed by means of special taxation. It has polluted the naturally clear water of these streams so as to render them wholly unfit to be used for any domestic or agricultural purposes by the adjacent proprietors. It has filled to a large extent, and is filling up the bed and narrowing the channels of these rivers, and the navigable bays into which they flow, thereby lessening and injuring their navigability, and impeding and endangering their navigation. All these effects have been constantly increasing during the past few years, and their still further increase is threatened by the continuance of the defendants' said mining operations. Held, that these acts, unless authorized by some law, constitute a public and private nuisance, destructive, continuous, increasing, and threatening to continue, increase, and be still more destructive.

During all this time the complainant was and he now is owner in fee of a block of buildings in Marysville, in the business portion of the city, about 500 feet from the levee on the Yuba. Originally the steam-boat landing for the city was on the Yuba, nearly opposite to this block, but by reason of the filling up of that river its navigation has been prevented, and the landing is now in the Feather, three-fourths of a mile distant from said block. By a break in the levee of the Yuba during one of its annual floods, the city of Marysville was inundated, the water stood several feet deep in this block, debris was deposited in it, its underpinning was washed out so that the roof fell in, and the repairs of these injuries cost between $2,000 and $3,000. The building is liable in the same manner to similar injuries from every flood in the river. The complainant, also owns two farms,—one of 952 acres, abutting on the Feather a few miles below Marysville, upon which there was formerly a public steam-boat landing for shipping and receiving freight and passengers, but which has become useless by the filling up of the river in front; the other of 720 acres, abutting on the opposite bank of the Feather. Seventy-five acres of one of these tracts and 50 acres of the other have been completely buried and destroyed by the debris, and the remaining portions are only protected from destruction by the levees, which on several occasions have broken, and the lands have been damaged by water charged with debris, and they are in danger of being overflowed and injured in a similar manner from a breach of the levees at any flood. The value of the complainant's land has been depreciated from these causes; his access, to the river from his farms for the purpose of shipping or receiving freights has been cut off; he has been obliged to pay an extraordinary, onerous, annual tax for the erection and maintenance of the levees to protect his property from the constantly increasing danger of loss or destruction. Held, that these facts constitute special injuries to the complainant, which entitle him to maintain a suit in equity to restrain the further commission of the public nuisance created by the defendants. ...

Hydraulic mining, as used in this opinion, is the process by which a bank of gold-bearing earth and rock is excavated by a jet of water, discharged through the converging nozzle of a pipe, under great pressure, the earth and debris being carried away by the same water, through sluices, and discharged on lower levels into the natural streams and water-courses below. Where the gravel or other material of the bank is cemented, or where the bank is composed of masses of pipeclay, it is shattered by blasting with powder, sometimes from 15 to 20 tons of powder being used at one blast to break up a bank. In the early periods of hydraulic mining, as in 1855, the water was discharged through a rubber or canvas hose, with nozzles of not more than an inch in diameter;

but later, upon the invention of the "Little Giant" and the "Monitor" machines, the size of the nozzle and the pressure were largely increased, till now the nozzle is from four to nine inches in diameter, discharging from 500 to 1,000 inches of water under a pressure of from three to four or five hundred feet.

For example, an eight-inch nozzle, at the North Bloomfield mine, discharges 185,000 cubic feet of water in an hour, with a velocity of 150 feet per second. The excavating power of such a body of water, discharged with such velocity, is enormous; and, unless the gravel is very heavy or firmly cemented, it is much in excess of its transporting power. At some of the mines, as at the North Bloomfield, several of these Monitors are worked, much of the time, night and day, the several levels upon which they are at work being brilliantly illuminated by electric lights, the electricity being generated by water power. A night scene of the kind, at the North Bloomfield mine, is in the highest degree weird and startling, and it cannot fail to strike strangers with wonder and admiration. The amount of debris discharged into the rivers by these operations can only be duly appreciated by actual observation. ...

The testimony shows that the expenses of this suit are paid by the anti-debris association, composed of the citizens of probably four or five counties affected by the nuisance; as Yuba, Sutter, Yolo, Sacramento, and doubtless part of Placer, the counties themselves also contributing; and that the expenses of the defense are paid by the "Miners' Association," composed of citizens of, and parties interested in, the several mining counties affected. It is, therefore, disguise it as we will, or technically call it what we may, and there can be no disputing the fact, a suit between the mining counties and valley counties interested in the great questions presented for decision. In view of the facts, is it not apparent that neither Woodruff nor any other one man, however large his property, could afford, unaided and alone, to enter into this litigation against the combined mining counties to redress his private grievances? Woodruff's interests involved are by no means insignificant, no matter how much may have been said to belittle them. His block of stores, built on one of the most eligible business locations in Marysville, at a cost of at least somewhere between $40,000 and $60,000, his nearly 1,000 acres of farming land—among the best in the state—in Sutter county, called the Hock Farm, and his Eliza tract of over 700 acres on the opposite side of the river, in Yuba county, and upon which a little settlement, embracing business houses and a public regular steam-boat landing, once existed, of which 125 acres in the aggregate on the two tracts are conceded to have been already destroyed certainly constitute an estate of no inconsiderable value. Yet it would manifestly, from what appears in this case, be better for him, pecuniarily, to see the whole absolutely destroyed, than alone, unaided by others, to attempt to maintain this litigation. ...

Undoubtedly, mining is an important industry in the state of California, and the state may, very properly, take any lawful measures within its power to encourage it, to the full extent, that it cap be carried on without injury to or the destruction of other industries or other rights, also important. It became patent to the most Casual observer that some plan must be devised by which hydraulic mining could be carried on without injury to the agricultural regions in the valleys, and without obstructing or destroying the use of the navigable waters of the state, or, in other words, without creating a grievous nuisance in the valleys below, or else that such mining must be stopped.

... After an examination of the great questions involved, as careful and thorough as we are capable of giving them, with a painfully anxious appreciation of the responsibilities resting upon us, and of the disastrous consequences to the defendants, we can come to no other conclusion than that complainant is entitled to a perpetual injunction.

8

Reflections

Charles Shinn's 1884 study of California mining camps and the Harvard philosopher Josiah Royce's 1886 history of California both cast the history of the state as a Whiggish story of successful political institution-building. The popular historian Hubert Howe Bancroft's history of California was likewise positive, although while Shinn and Royce described a procession from chaos to order, for the crowd-pleasing Bancroft, California's history merely moved from good to even better. In different ways, Shinn, Royce, and Bancroft were able to elide the violence and instability of the gold rush.

38

CHARLES HOWARD SHINN

Mining Camps: A Study in American Frontier Government

1884

Born in 1852, Shinn, like the better-known Frederick Jackson Turner, the author of the influential frontier thesis, studied History at Johns Hopkins University under the historian Herbert Baxter Adams. While Turner's frontier thesis located American democracy in the transformation of wilderness to civilization, Shinn adopted Adams's "germ theory" of history. According to this theory, democracy sprang from Teutonic "germs"

Charles Howard Shinn, *Mining Camps: A Study in American Frontier Government* (New York: Charles Scribner's Sons, 1884), 13–136.

rooted in Germanic tribes and found its fullest expressions among those tribespeople's Anglo-Saxon descendants in England and the United States. Shinn extended his mentor's theories to California.

The mining-camps, whose white tents and rude cabins rose so rapidly beside these rivers ... have found an enduring place in literature. The Argonaut himself has become one of the heroic figures of the past, and is likely enough to survive, as real and strong a type in the story of America as Viking or Crusader in that of Europe. But it is the place held by the Argonaut as an organizer of society, that is most important. He often appears in literature as a dialect-speaking rowdy, savagely picturesque, rudely turbulent: in reality, he was a plain American citizen cut loose from authority, freed from the restraints and protections of law, and forced to make the defence and organization of society a part of his daily business. In its best estate, the mining-camp of California was a manifestation of the inherent capacities of the race for self-government. That political instinct, deep rooted in Lex Saxonum, to blossom in Magna Charta and in English unwritten constitution, has seldom in modern times afforded a finer illustration of its seemingly inexhaustible force. Here, in a new land, under new conditions, subjected to tremendous pressure and strain, but successfully resisting them, were associated bodies of freemen bound together for a time by common interests, ruled by equal laws, and owning allegiance to no higher authority than their own sense of right and wrong. They held meetings, chose officers, decided disputes, meted out a stern and swift punishment to offenders, and managed their local affairs with entire success; and the growth of their communities was proceeding at such a rapid rate, that days and weeks were often sufficient for vital changes, which, in more staid communities, would have required months or even years. ...

Each community, once welded together in camp-life, possesses a unity of feeling that bids fair to be permanent. This is true of California, and may reasonably be expected to prove true of the later-settled mining-regions. We observe, in the newest camps of the British-Columbia border, the same spirit of swift, healthy camp-life, the same return to primitive forms of jurisprudence, the same American determination that crime shall be punished, property and life made safe: therefore we may have faith that the same results will follow there as in California, that stable communities will be established, and higher forms of society evolved.

39

JOSIAH ROYCE

California, from the Conquest in 1846 to the Second Vigilance Committee in San Francisco: A Study of American Character

1886

Royce was born in Grass Valley, California, in 1855. He studied at the University of California before moving to Johns Hopkins University, where he received a doctorate in philosophy in 1878. He became a professor of philosophy at Harvard in 1882.

[T]he better part of every ... mining community learned, from all this disorder, the sad lesson that their stay in California was to be long, their social responsibility great, and their duty to devote time and money to rational work as citizens unavoidable. They saw the fearful effects of their own irresponsible freedom. They began to form town governments of a more stable sort, to condemn rather than to excuse mob violence, to regard the free and adventurous prospecting life, if pursued on a grand scale, as a dangerous and generally profitless waste of the community's energies, to prefer thereto steady work in great mining enterprises, and in every way to insist upon order. ... The romantic degradation of the early mining life, with its transient glory, its fatal fascination, its inevitable brutality, and its resulting loathsome corruption, gave place to the commonplace industries of the later mining days. The quartz mines and the deep placers were in time developed, vast amounts of capital came to be invested in the whole mining industry, and in a few years (by 1858, for instance) many mining towns were almost as conservative as much older manufacturing towns have been in other States. ... [T]he moral elasticity of our people is so great, their social vitality so marvelous, that a community of Americans could sin as fearfully as, in the early years, the mining community did sin, and yet could live to purify itself within

Josiah Royce, *California, from the Conquest in 1846 to the Second Vigilance Committee in San Francisco: A Study of American Character* (Boston: Houghton Mifflin, 1886), 375–76, 499–501.

so short a time, not by revolution, but by a simple progress from social foolishness to social steadfastness. ...

The race that has grown up in California, as the outcome of these early struggles, is characterized by very marked qualities of strength and weakness, some of which, perchance, even a native Californian like the author, who neither can nor would outgrow his healthy local traits, may still be able to note and confess. A general sense of social irresponsibility is, even to-day, the average Californian's easiest failing. Like his father, he is probably a born wanderer, who will feel as restless in his farm life, or in his own town, as his father felt in his. He will have little or no sense of social or material barriers, he will perchance hunt for himself a new home somewhere else in the world, or in the old home will long for some speculative business that promises easy wealth, or again, on the other hand, he will undertake some great material labor that attracts him by its imposing difficulty. ... In short, the Californian has too often come to love mere fullness of life, and to lack reverence for the relations of life.

...It is the State, the Social Order, that is divine. We are all but dust, save as this social order gives us life. When we think it our instrument, our plaything, and make our private fortunes the one object, then this social order rapidly becomes vile to us; we call it sordid, degraded, corrupt, unspiritual, and ask how we may escape from it forever. But if we turn again and serve the social order, and not merely ourselves, we soon find that what we are serving is simply our own highest spiritual destiny in bodily form. It is never truly sordid or corrupt or unspiritual; it is only we that are so when we neglect our duty.

40

HUBERT HOWE BANCROFT

History of California

1890

Bancroft was born in Granville, Ohio, in 1832. He moved to California in 1852 to manage a bookstore; in 1868 he turned from selling books

Hubert Howe Bancroft, *History of California*, vol. 7 (San Francisco: The History Company, 1890), 755–57.

to writing them. His production was prodigious — in large part because
he employed scores of assistants who wrote the actual text that Bancroft
compiled and edited.

Notwithstanding some drawbacks, few who have become accustomed
to the stir and excitement of California life, to the glories of her scenery and climate, to her boundless opportunities, her wonderful prosperity, would care to exchange for any other the land of their nativity
or adoption. It is now little more than four decades since the discovery
of gold attracted to this coast the attention of the civilized world, and
during that period, little more than the span of a single generation, how
marvellous the transformation that many yet living have witnessed! As
at the touch of a fairy's wand, the land has been converted from one
vast pasture-ground into a region smiling with grain-fields, orchards,
and vineyards, from the southern boundary of the state to the valleys
overshadowed by the snow-capped peaks of Shasta, and from the shores
of ocean to the foothills of the Sierra.

He who would know the utmost that can be accomplished by the
energy and intelligence of man should study the history of this state, for
nowhere else can be found such comprehensiveness of plan, such bold-
ness of emprise, such skill and daring in execution. If as yet we lack the
minuteness and thoroughness of eastern and European communities,
here are to be found in some departments the most remarkable achieve-
ments that have ever been witnessed in the world's industrial career.
Here are the largest wheat and dairy farms, the largest stock-farms, the
largest vineyards, orchards, and orange-groves, the largest hydraulic-
mines, the largest mining-ditches, the most powerful mining-pumps and
mining machinery, the highest aqueduct, the largest lumber-flume, and
one at least of the largest saw-mills in the United States, or in any country on earth. And yet what has already come to pass, how wonderful so
ever in our sight, is but an earnest of what may be expected when there
are hands enough for the work to be done, and consumers enough for
its products.

And to what is California indebted for the position which she holds
to-day as the first state in the union in her product of gold and wine and
fruit, as the first in variety of agricultural products, as the first in wealth
per capita, changing the financial conditions of the world by her enormous yield of the precious metals, changing the conditions of labor, and
giving to commerce stimulus and direction? To the genius and enterprise of her inhabitants must these results be ascribed, for whatever has

been found most excellent in other lands has been adopted in this state. Nowhere else has been displayed such aptitude in studying and applying the lessons of experience; nowhere has such progress been made in new directions; nowhere have so many appliances been successfully brought to bear on the development of agriculture and mining; nowhere is there so much of pride, and of excusable pride, among her adopted no less than her native-born citizens.

It seems but as yesterday since the Pacific coast metropolis was but a collection of cabins and tents clustering among the few level acres of ground that skirted the waters of the bay, the mud-flats and sand-dunes, the steep, rocky hills, and the swamp-covered ravines. Never, perhaps, was a more unpromising site selected, and never did skill and enterprise achieve so quick and complete a mastery over the obstacles of nature. To-day those hills and ravines are covered with a city of over 300,000 inhabitants, stretching forth east and north to the shores of the harbor, westward almost to the Pacific, and southward beyond the Mission hills, where in pioneer times the only wagon-road passed through miles of loose and shifting sand. Here have been erected some of the finest public and business buildings, some of the most tasteful and commodious residences in the United States; here is one, at least, of the largest, and more than one of the best-appointed hotels and restaurants; here are theatres, churches, schools, and libraries such as are seldom found in cities of equal size; here are facilities for commerce, for travel, and communication such as are excelled by few eastern or old-world centres.

And what will be the condition of this state a few generations hence, when the moral and political status of the community shall be on a par with her material greatness; when trickery and demagogism shall give place to honest and enlightened statesmanship; when manly worth and intellectual culture shall be recognized; and when from the heterogeneous elements of which our western commonwealth is composed shall be eliminated their impurities and debasing influences? Here, let us hope, will be the favored land, where social science will find its most fitting sphere; here the accumulations gathered in the vast store house of human experience; here the abode of all that is best worth preserving in the art, the science, the literature of the world; and here, if California be true to herself and her higher destiny, may be found one of the highest forms of development of which humanity is capable.

A Chronology of the California Gold Rush (1572–1885)

1542   Juan Rodríguez Cabrillo explores the coast of California.

1769   *July 16*   Father Junípero Serra establishes the first Franciscan mission in California, at San Diego.

1784   *August 28*   Junípero Serra dies, having founded nine missions along the California coast.

1821   *August 24*   Mexico becomes independent of Spain according to the Treaty of Córdoba.

1824   *August 18*   Colonization Act authorizes Mexico to make large land grants to *empresarios* who will sponsor immigration to California.

1828   Prospectors discover gold in northwest Georgia.

1833   *August 17*   Secularization Act authorizes Mexico to confiscate mission lands in California.

1835   President Jackson offers Mexico $500,000 for San Francisco Bay.

1839   *June 18*   John Sutter receives a 50,000-acre land grant near present-day Sacramento.

1845   *August*   John Frémont's exploring party leaves Bent's Fort in Colorado.

        December 10   Frémont reaches Sutter's Fort.

        December 29   The United States annexes the Republic of Texas.

1846   *April 25*   American troops and Mexican cavalry clash between the Nueces River and the Rio Grande. The United States had provoked the conflict with Mexico by sending troops south of the Nueces River—the recognized southern boundary of Texas—to the Rio Grande, which the United States claimed as the southern boundary of the new state.

        May 8   Archibald Gillespie, a Marine lieutenant, locates Frémont in Oregon and delivers him orders to use his small force to secure California for the U.S.

May 13 The United States declares war on Mexico.

June Frémont attacks Indians in California whom he believes are allies of the Mexicans.

June 14 About thirty American immigrants in California capture the commander of the Mexican presidio in Sonoma and declare a California republic.

June 15 The United States agrees to divide the Oregon country with Great Britain.

July Frémont's force is absorbed into the U.S. military.

July 31 Samuel Brannan, an elder of the Mormon Church, lands at Yerba Buena (later San Francisco) with 250 Mormon followers. A year later, he meets with Brigham Young and tries to persuade Young to make California the primary destination for Mormon settlers, but Young opts for Utah.

September 29 Californios under José Maria Flores force the U.S. garrison to retreat from Los Angeles.

1847 *January 8* American forces under Commodore Robert Stockton and General Stephen Kearney defeat Flores near Los Angeles, effectively ending Californio resistance.

1848 *January 24* James Marshall discovers gold on the South Fork of the American River.

February 2 Mexico cedes California and what becomes the states of Nevada, Utah, Colorado, Arizona, and New Mexico to the United States according to the Treaty of Guadalupe Hidalgo, ending the Mexican–American War.

March–December Roughly 20,000 people, primarily from northern Mexico, journey to California to prospect for gold.

December 5 President Polk appends a report from Richard Mason, the military governor of California, detailing the discovery of gold in California, to his annual report to Congress.

November 1 John A. Sutter, Jr. announces a plan to build Sacramento City.

1849 Between 25,000 and 30,000 Americans travel overland to California.

September–October Delegates meet in Monterey to draft a constitution for California.

1850 *August* "Squatters Riot" in Sacramento.

September 9 California is admitted to the United States as the thirty-first state.

October Cholera breaks out in Sacramento and elsewhere in California.

1851   *March*   The United States Land Commission begins its review of Mexican land grants.

May   Gold is discovered in Australia. Eight thousand Americans travel to Australia to prospect for gold.

June   First San Francisco Vigilance Committee is constituted.

1852   Miners in California begin using pressurized water—hydraulic mining—to flush gold-bearing gravel into a sluice box.

1856   *June–August*   Second San Francisco Vigilance Committee.

1860   *February 26*   Massacre of Wiyots at Indian Island in northern California.

1862   *July 1*   President Lincoln signs the Pacific Railway Act, authorizing the construction of a transcontinental railroad.

1863   Two-year-long drought begins in southern California.

Construction on the Central Pacific Railroad, moving eastward from Sacramento, begins. By 1868, 12,000 immigrant Chinese workers are employed in construction.

1869   *May 10*   The Central Pacific links with the Union Pacific, completing the transcontinental railroad.

December   Modoc leader Captain Jack agrees to remove from the Modocs' territory in northeastern California to a reservation in Oregon.

1870   The California State Board of Forestry reports that since 1850 one-third of the available timber in the state has been cut.

April   Finding conditions on the reservation intolerable, Captain Jack leads most of the Modocs back to their lands in California.

1871   Timber producers in coastal northern California form a cartel, the Redwood Lumber Association, in an attempt to fix the price of redwood lumber.

1872   *November*   The U.S. Army attacks Captain Jack's camp, starting the Modoc War. The Modocs take refuge in the lava beds south of Tule Lake.

1873   *April*   Captain Jack murders General Edward Canby during a negotiation for a truce to end the Modoc War.

May   Captain Jack is betrayed by other Modocs and captured by the U.S. Army.

October Captain Jack is hanged.

1878   *February*   Farmers and miners testify before a committee of California state legislators about the hydraulic mining "debris question."

1882   *May 6*   Chinese Exclusion Act.

1884　*January 7*　Lorenzo Sawyer's ruling in *Woodruff* v. *North Bloomfield Gravel Mining Co.* bans hydraulic mining in the California gold country.

1885　*February*　One thousand whites expel just over one hundred Chinese residents from Eureka. Similar expulsions follow in thirty-five California cities and towns over the next year.

Questions for Consideration

1. How did the first observers of the Gold Rush understand the search for gold? How accurate were those first descriptions? How did the perspectives of observers such as Sherman, Mason, and Clapp differ from those of miners such as Smith, Powell, and Chaffee (Documents 1–6)?

2. What difference did it make to prospectors that California was transferred from Mexican to American control just as gold was discovered (Document 3)?

3. Why were relations between Indians and whites in California so characterized by violence (Documents 23–26)?

4. Why were white Californians so opposed to the presence of African-American laborers, either slave or free, in the state (Documents 13–14)?

5. Were the rights of those who had received land grants in California from the Mexican government adequately respected by United States legal authorities after 1850? Explain your answer (Documents 19–20).

6. Charles Robinson, advocating for squatters rights, charged that John Sutter's vague land grant that he had received from a Mexican governor of California did not preclude squatters from staking a claim to the land (Document 9). John Hittell pointed to the problems that squatters posed to those who had received land grants under Mexican rule (Document 20). How could the rights of both squatters and those who had received grants have been respected?

7. In what ways did white miners exploit the privileges of their race (Documents 15, 23–26, 27–29)?

8. Why were cities in Gold Rush California such as Sacramento and San Francisco so characterized by violence (Documents 8, 9, 12)?

9. In the nineteenth-century West, many mineral rushes created brief spasms of settlement, but most sites were quickly abandoned after the mines had played out (Document 7). Why did California continue to develop and grow as the mines diminished in profitability (Documents 32, 38–40)?

10. Why were whites in California so hostile to Chinese immigrants? What tactics did they use to harass and suppress the Chinese (Documents 27–30)?

11. In what ways was the California Gold Rush a transnational event? How does this change our understanding of the Gold Rush (Documents 15–17)?

12. How does taking the environmental costs of hydraulic mining into account change the reckoning of the economic effects of the gold rush (Documents 33–36)?

13. Why did a federal judge prohibit hydraulic mining in 1884 (Document 37)?

14. By the 1880s, how did historians' understanding of the significance of the Gold Rush differ from that of gold rush participants (Documents 38–40)?

Selected Bibliography

Blodgett, Peter J. *Land of Golden Dreams: California in the Gold Rush Decade, 1848–1858*. San Marino, CA: Huntington Library, 1999.

Eifler, Mark A. *Gold Rush Capitalists: Greed and Growth in Sacramento*. Albuquerque: University of New Mexico Press, 2002.

Ethington, Philip J. *The Public City: The Political Construction of Urban Life in San Francisco, 1850–1900*. New York: Cambridge University Press, 1994.

Greenberg, Amy S. *A Wicked War: Polk, Clay, Lincoln, and the 1846 U.S. Invasion of Mexico*. New York: Knopf, 2012.

Gutiérrez, Ramón A., and Richard J. Orsi, eds. *Contested Eden: California Before the Gold Rush*. Berkeley: University of California Press, 1998.

Hackel, Steven W. *Children of Coyote, Missionaries of Saint Francis: Indian-Spanish Relations in Colonial California, 1769–1850*. Chapel Hill: University of North Carolina Press, 2005.

Holliday, J. S. *Rush for Riches: Gold Fever and the Making of California*. Berkeley: University of California Press, 1999.

Hurtado, Albert L. *Indian Survival on the California Frontier*. New Haven, CT: Yale University Press, 1988.

———. *Intimate Frontiers: Sex, Gender, and Culture in Old California*. Albuquerque: University of New Mexico Press, 1999.

———. *John Sutter: A Life on the North American Frontier*. Norman: University of Oklahoma Press, 2006.

Isenberg, Andrew C. *Mining California: An Ecological History*. New York: Hill and Wang, 2005.

———. "Mercurial Nature: The California Gold Country and the Coal Fields of the Ruhr Basin, 1850–1900." In Ursula Lehmkuhl and Hermann Wellenreuther, eds., *Historians and Nature: Comparative Approaches to Environmental History*. Oxford: Berg, 2007: 125–45.

———. "Between Mexico and the United States: From *Indios* to Vaqueros in the Pastoral Borderlands." In John Tutino, ed., *Mexico and Mexicans in the Making of the United States*. Austin: University of Texas Press, 2012: 85–109.

Johnson, Susan L. *Roaring Camp: The Social World of the California Gold Rush*. New York: Norton, 2000.

Kelley, Robert L. *Gold vs. Grain: The Hydraulic Mining Controversy in California's Sacramento Valley*. Glendale, CA: Arthur H. Clark, 1959.

McEvoy, Arthur F. *The Fisherman's Problem Ecology and Law in the California Fisheries, 1850–1980*. New York: Cambridge University Press, 1986.

McGuinness, Aims. *Path of Empire: Panama and the California Gold Rush*. Ithaca, NY: Cornell University Press, 2008.

Ngai, Mae M. "Chinese Gold Miners and the 'Chinese Question' in Nineteenth-Century California and Victoria." *Journal of American History*, 101 (March 2015): 44–70.

Owens, Kenneth N., ed. *Riches for All: The California Gold Rush and the World*. Lincoln: University of Nebraska Press, 2002.

Paul, Rodman. *California Gold: The Beginning of Mining in the Far West*. Cambridge, MA: Harvard University Press, 1947.

Pisani, Donald. "Squatter Law in California, 1850–1858." *Western Historical Quarterly*, 25 (Autumn 1994): 277–310.

Pitt, Leonard. *The Decline of the Californios: A Social History of the Spanish-Speaking Californians, 1846–1890*. Berkeley: University of California Press, 1966.

Rawls, James J., and Richard J. Orsi, eds. *A Golden State: Mining and Economic Development in Gold Rush California*. Berkeley: University of California Press, 1998.

Rohrbough, Malcolm. *Days of Gold: The California Gold Rush and the American Nation*. Berkeley: University of California Press, 1997.

Saxton, Alexander. *The Indispensable Enemy: Labor and the Anti-Chinese Movement in California*. Berkeley: University of California Press, 1971.

Shelton, Tamara V. *A Squatter's Republic: Land and the Politics of Monopoly in California, 1850–1900*. Berkeley: University of California Press, 2013.

Starr, Kevin, and Richard J. Orsi, eds. *Rooted in Barbarous Soil: People, Culture, and Community in Gold Rush California*. Berkeley: University of California Press, 2000.

Unruh, John D., Jr. *The Plains Across: The Overland Emigrants and the Trans-Mississippi West, 1840–60*. Urbana: University of Illinois Press, 1979.

Vaught, David. *After the Gold Rush: Tarnished Dreams in the Sacramento Valley*. Baltimore, MD: Johns Hopkins University Press, 2007.

Weber, David. *The Spanish Frontier in North America*. New Haven, CT: Yale University Press, 1994.

White, Richard. "The Gold Rush: Consequences and Contingencies." *California History*, 77 (Spring 1998): 42–55.

Index